SECOND EDITION

AURALLY CODED ENGLISH

ACE SPELLING ACTIVITIES

DAVID MOSELEY AND GWYN SINGLETON

OVER 100 PHOTOCOPIABLE ACTIVITY SHEETS FOR USE WITH THE *ACE SPELLING DICTIONARY*

FIND WORDS **QUICKLY** AND **IMPROVE** YOUR SPELLING

ACE Spelling Activities (second edition)

ISBN: 978-1-85503-594-2

© David Moseley and Gwyn Singleton 2016
Illustrations by Yuliya Somina/Beehive Illustration

First edition published 1993
This edition published 2016
10 9 8 7 6 5 4

Printed in the UK by Page Bros (Norwich) Ltd
Cover design by Jason Roberts for View Creative Design Agency
Text design and typeset by Andy Wilson for Green Desert Ltd

LDA, 2 Gregory Street, Hyde, Cheshire, SK14 4HR

www.ldalearning.com

The right of David Moseley and Gwyn Singleton to be identified
as the authors of this work has been asserted in accordance with
Sections 77 and 78 of the Copyright, Designs and Patents Act 1988.

All rights reserved. This book contains materials which may be
reproduced by photocopier or other means for use by the purchaser.
The permission is granted on the understanding that these copies
will be used within the educational establishment of the purchaser.
The book and all its contents remain copyright. Copies may be made
without reference to the publisher or the licensing scheme for the
making of photocopies operated by the Publishers Licensing Society.

Contents

Preface v

Introducing ACE

Counting syllables	1
Learning how to use the *ACE Spelling Dictionary* in three easy lessons	2
More word-finding practice	13

Using ACE

Spellings for sounds	18
Spellings for sounds puzzles	50
Car registration games	61
Tricky word endings	64
Doubles or singles	68
Find the middle syllable	70
Find the two middle syllables	81
Words within words	83
Find the baseword or root	85
Introducing the parts of speech	87
Searching for patterns	93

Learning spellings

Words you need to know	94
Learn to spell these really useful words	97
Slippery Characters	109

Answers 121

All ACE Spelling Activities are suitable for individual work and for working under guidance in pairs or groups. As shown below, many can also be organised as class activities, provided that enough copies of the *ACE Spelling Dictionary* are available.

Activity	Pages	Starting age	Suitable for class work
Counting syllables	1	6	C
Learning how to use the *ACE Spelling Dictionary* in three easy lessons	2–12	6	C*
More word-finding practice	13–17	7	C*
Spellings for sounds	18–49	8	
Spellings for sounds puzzles	50–60	8	
Car registration games	61–63	8	C*
Tricky word endings	64–67	9	C*
Doubles or singles	68–69	9	C*
Find the middle syllable	70–80	9	C*
Find the two middle syllables	81–82	10	C*
Words within words	83–84	8	
Find the baseword or root	85–86	9	C
Introducing the parts of speech	87–92	9	C*
Searching for patterns	93	10	C
Words you need to know	94–96	8	C
Learn to spell these really useful words	97–108	7	
Slippery Characters	109–120	7	

*If these activities are to be done on a class basis, each person will need access to the *ACE Spelling Dictionary*.
All answers can be found on pages 121–143.

Preface

The *ACE Spelling Dictionary* was first published in 1986 and *ACE Spelling Activities* in 1993. Both consistently receive five-star reviews from home and school users who need to check spellings quickly. *ACE Spelling Activities* takes learners beyond looking up words to studying spellings and learning from personal lists. It is designed for users aged seven and above and provides a framework for all learners to get to grips with phonics and the English spelling system. Whilst especially valuable for dyslexic pupils, the ACE resources are designed to improve spelling and writing performance on a whole-school basis.

The 2015 edition of *ACE Spelling Activities* has been slightly adjusted to match the latest revisions of the *ACE Spelling Dictionary*, and a few rather dated references have been replaced. More importantly, the activities now fully cover the English statutory Spelling Lists for Years 3–6. There is a new six-page section, called Slippery Characters, which focuses on 240 frequently misspelt words between five and 13 letters in length. This provides practice in quickly finding words in a syllable column on a specified page of the *ACE Spelling Dictionary* and draws attention to the most tricky parts of word spellings. If words selected from this activity are studied and systematically learned, many misspellings which often persist for a lifetime can be avoided.

Introducing ACE

Counting syllables

Aim: The student should be able to say how many syllables there are in any spoken word (up to four syllables).

The teacher can work with a group or whole class, asking for individual or group responses. In one-to-one work a partner or teaching assistant can read out the words and say whether the responses are correct. The following three stages should be followed.

1 The teacher or tutor (**T**) says a word slowly and taps out the syllables at the same time. The student repeats the word and taps out the syllables. **T** asks 'How many taps?'. This should be done with the following words.

play-ground	win-dow	ba-na-na	mud	un-for-tu-nate
TAP-TAP	TAP-TAP	TAP-TAP-TAP	TAP	TAP-TAP-TAP-TAP

Repeat more slowly if necessary, with the words in a different order.

2 **T** says a word without tapping and asks the student to repeat the word and tap it out. Each time, **T** asks 'How many taps?'. This is done with words from the following list until ten words are tapped out correctly.

***	newspaper	**	picture	*	paint	****	television
**	spider	*	mice	**	monster	***	dinosaur
**	postman	**	burglar	***	acrobat	****	politician
**	pancake	***	margarine	****	supermarket	**	kitchen
*	crash	****	helicopter	**	rocket	***	motorbike

3 **T** says a word and simply asks 'How many syllables?'. This is done, taking words at random from the list below, until a success rate of 19/20 is obtained.

**	money	*	shop	**	birthday	**	present
**	bedroom	*	door	***	wallpaper	*	stairs
***	holidays	*	weeks	***	underground	****	underwater
***	crocodile	****	alligator	*	shark	**	danger
****	caterpillar	*	moth	***	butterfly	*	eggs
**	rabbit	****	invisible	*	hat	**	magic
*	win	***	manager	**	football	****	competition
****	everybody	**	children	**	mother	***	grandfather
*	clock	**	morning	***	afternoon	***	yesterday
****	mysterious	***	horrible	***	beautiful	***	exciting

© David Moseley and Gwyn Singleton 2015 | *ACE Spelling Activities* | LDA | Permission to photocopy

Introducing ACE

Learning how to use the *ACE Spelling Dictionary* in three easy lessons

The *ACE Spelling Dictionary* improves spelling and enhances linguistic awareness at all levels of the National Curriculum.

Teachers who adopt the *ACE Spelling Dictionary* for class use are often surprised that their students find it so easy. As soon as students succeed in finding words, the advantages of the Dictionary become self-evident.

The 30-second guide to the *ACE Spelling Dictionary* found on the inside front cover of the Dictionary is an excellent introduction, especially when each student has a copy of the Dictionary. However, this initial demonstration does need to be followed up by practice with the Index page, covering the sounds in each section, and looking up words in the Dictionary itself.

The following three lessons provide the necessary practice and are suitable for both small groups and whole classes. After following three lessons of direct instruction and practice, students should be able to find ten words in under five minutes and should then progress to an average speed of 20 seconds per word.

When introducing the Dictionary on a class basis, at least one copy per table is needed. Each of the lessons covers sounds from different sections of the Index – photocopy masters of these sections are provided so that each student can have their own copy to work with. Teachers may like to make digital copies of these to use in whole-class tuition.

Lesson 1

Introducing ACE

Aims: The student should be able to:

a) identify long vowel sounds in a selection of words

b) use the long vowel sounds part of the Index to find the page numbers for a selection of words

c) look up words in the darker blue part of the dictionary.

1 Begin with listening and speaking activities, starting with the long vowel animal names: **snail**, **eagle**, **lion**, **goat** and **newt**.

Ask the students if they can hear certain vowel sounds in each of these animal names. Use correct and incorrect vowel sounds, for example, 'Can you hear /**ae**/ in **snail**?', 'Can you hear /**ee**/ in **snail**?'

Make the vowel sounds longer and louder if you need to.

Continue until responses are confident and correct and then move on to identifying long vowel sounds in other words. For example, 'Can you hear /**ee**/ in **fine**?', 'Can you hear /**ae**/ in **baby**?'.

Again, continue until responses are confident and correct.

Selecting a long vowel sound, ask students if they can hear the sound in a variety of words. For example, 'Can you hear /**ae**/ in **pail**, **sail**, **tail**, **tile**?'.

Finally, ask students to give you the vowel sound they can hear in the long vowel animal names, giving a choice of three. For example, 'What is the vowel sound in **snail**: /**ae**/, /**ee**/ or /**ie**/?'. Continue with different animals and three vowel sound choices until the sounds in all the long vowel animal names are correctly identified.

2 Practise using the Index to find page numbers. Each student should have a copy of the long vowel part in the middle of the Index (see Index 1 on page 5). Teachers may also like to make a digital copy for class tuition.

Beginning with the animal picture words, ask students first to point to the snail picture next to the letters 'ae' which stand for the sound /**ae**/. Ask which letter **snail** begins with and have them find the letter 'S' in the alphabet across the top of the page. Then, show them how to move one finger along the line of page numbers from /**ae**/ and the other finger down from 'S', until they meet at a page number. **Snail** is on page 149!

Repeat this exercise with **eagle**, **lion**, **goat** and **newt**. You may need to prompt students with the vowel sound initially, but continue the exercise until the page numbers can be found by the students themselves.

Once students can readily achieve this, ask them to find the page numbers for the following animal words: **ape**, **beaver**, **bison**, **mule**, **poodle**, **reindeer**, **sheep**, **snake**, **tiger**, **whale**.

This time they will need to identify the spelling picture for the vowel sound first. For example, what is the first vowel sound in **tiger**? It is /**ie**/, which is the same as in **lion**.

Introducing ACE

Use these topic lists until students have mastered using Index 1 to find page numbers.

bacon, cake, cereal, cheese, doughnut, mousse, pie, steak, trifle, tuna

beans, beetroot, coleslaw, cucumber, leeks, maize, peanuts, peas, seaweed, swede

apricot, coconut, dates, grapefruit, lime, peach, pineapple, prunes, raisins, rhubarb

basin, bowl, knife, ladle, microwave, plate, scales, soap, teapot, toast

3 Practise looking up words from the above lists or elsewhere in the darker blue part of the Dictionary. After turning to the page, say the word in distinct syllables and have the class say, tap and count the syllables. Make sure they look in the correct column and, if there is a homonym, that they check the meaning. Where the word is not given in plural form (e.g. prune), an 's' should be added. Note that in one case (swede) the target word is in a section which continues for three pages.

Introducing ACE

Index 1

		A	B	C	D	E	F	G	H	I	J	K	L	M	N	O	P	Q	R	S	T	U	V	W	X	Y	Z		
LONG VOWEL	ae	137	138	139	140	141	142	143	144	144	145	145	146	146	147	147	148	148	149	151	151	151	152	—	152	—	ae	BABY SNAIL
LONG VOWEL	ee	153	154	155	156	157	158	159	160	161	162	162	163	164	165	165	166	167	167	169	172	—	173	174	—	175	175	ee	BREEDING EAGLE
LONG VOWEL	ie	176	177	178	178	180	181	182	182	183	184	184	185	186	187	187	188	189	189	190	192	—	193	193	194	—	194	ie	LIVELY LION
LONG VOWEL	oe	195	195	196	197	197	198	199	200	200	201	201	201	202	202	203	204	206	206	207	208	208	208	209	—	209	209	oe	LONELY GOAT
LONG VOWELS	ue oo	210 211	211 212	212 213	213 213	214 214	214 215	215 216	216 216	216 217	217 218	218 219	219 220	220 221	221 222	222 223	223 223	223 224	224									ue oo	SMOOTH NEWT

© David Moseley and Gwyn Singleton 2015 | *ACE Spelling Activities* | LDA | Permission to photocopy

Lesson 2

Introducing ACE

Aims: The student should be able to:
a) identify short vowel sounds in a selection of words
b) use the short vowel sound part of the Index to find the page numbers for a selection of words
c) look up words in the first two parts of the Dictionary.

1. Begin with listening and speaking activities, starting with the short vowel animal names: **cat**, **elephant**, **pig**, **dog**, **duck** and **woodpecker**.

   Ask the students if they can hear certain vowel sounds in each of these animal names, for example, 'Can you hear /**a**/ in **cat**?', 'Can you hear /**e**/ in **pig**?'.

   Make the vowel sounds longer and louder if you need to.

   Continue until responses are confident and correct and then move on to identifying short vowel sounds in other words. For example, 'Can you hear /**a**/ in **active**?', 'Can you hear /**i**/ in **big**?'.

   Again, continue until responses are confident and correct.

   Selecting a short vowel sound, ask students if they can hear the sound in a variety of words. For example, 'Can you hear /**a**/ in **pat**, **fat**, **mat**, **pet**?'.

   Finally, ask students to give you the vowel sound they can hear in the short vowel animal names, giving a choice of three. For example, 'What is the vowel sound in **cat**: /**ae**/, /**a**/ or /**e**/?'. Continue with the different animals and three vowel sound choices until the sounds in all the short vowel names are correctly identified.

2. Practise using the Index to find page numbers first for short and then for both short and long vowel words. Each student should have a copy of the first two parts of the Index (see Index 2 on page 8). Teachers may also like to make a digital copy for class tuition.

   Beginning with the animal picture words, ask students first to point to the cat picture next to the letter 'a', which stands for the sound /**a**/. Ask which letter **cat** begins with and have them find the letter 'C' in the alphabet across the top of the page. Then, show them how to move one finger along the line of page numbers from /**a**/ and the other finger down from 'C', until they meet at a page number. **Cat** is on page 7!

   Repeat this exercise with **duck**, **pig**, **watchful** and **woodpecker**. You may need to prompt students with the vowel sounds initially, but continue the exercise until the page numbers can be found by the students themselves.

   Once students can readily achieve this, ask them to find the page numbers for the following animal words: **camel, donkey, frog, hedgehog, kangaroo, leopard, monkey, pigeon, rabbit, rook**.

   This time they will need to identify the spelling picture for the vowel sound first. For example, what is the first vowel sound in **rabbit**? It is /**a**/, which is the same as in **cat**.

Introducing ACE

Use these topic lists until students have mastered using Index 2 to find page numbers.

biscuit, bread, butter, chicken, chocolate, crisps, eggs, haddock, jam, popcorn

broccoli, cabbage, cauliflower, celery, lettuce, mushroom, onion, pepper, pumpkin, spinach

apple, blackberry, cherry, damson, fig, lemon, melon, orange, plum, tangerine

bottle, brush, clock, fridge, matches, mirror, rack, scissors, sieve, whisk

After working with Index 2, ask students to find the page numbers for both short and long vowel words from the following lists. If there is any confusion between short and long vowels, ask, for example, 'Is it short /a/ as in **cat**, or long /ae/ as in **snail**?' as appropriate.

black, blue, buff, crimson, gold, green, indigo, red, ruby, white

apron, boots, collar, dress, jeans, nightdress, shoes, sweater, tie, vest

bicycle, boat, glider, helicopter, motorcycle, scooter, submarine, train, van, yacht

bus, coach, cycle, ferry, hovercraft, liner, lorry, rocket, tricycle, truck

chewing, cooking, drinking, eating, helping, listening, nodding, sleeping, watching, writing

baker, bricklayer, cook, miner, optician, sailor, scientist, secretary, soldier, teacher

3 Practise looking up words from the above lists or elsewhere in the Dictionary. After turning to the page, say the word in distinct syllables and have the class say, tap and count the syllables. Make sure they look in the correct column and, if there is a homonym, that they check the meaning. Note that in some cases (apple, biscuit, bus, butter, crimson, drinking, fridge, indigo, matches, optician, orange, spinach, sweater) the target word is in a section which continues for two or more pages.

Index 2

Introducing ACE

	A	B	C	D	E	F	G	H	I	J	K	L	M	N	O	P	Q	R	S	T	U	V	W	X	Y	Z	
SHORT VOWEL **a**	1	5	7	10	11	12	14	16	17	18	18	19	20	21	–	22	24	24	25	28	29	29	30	–	30	30	**a** ACTIVE CAT
SHORT VOWEL **e**	31	32	33	34	36	39	39	40	41	42	42	43	44	45	45	46	47	48	50	52	53	53	54	54	55	55	**e** HEALTHY ELEPHANT
SHORT VOWEL **i**	56	57	59	61	65	68	70	71	72	77	78	79	80	81	81	82	83	84	87	90	91	91	92	–	–	93	**i** BIG PIGLET
SHORT VOWEL **o**	94	95	96	99	99	100	101	102	102	103	103	104	105	105	106	108	109	110	111	113	113	114	114	–	115	115	**o** WATCHFUL DOG
SHORT VOWELS **u oo**	116	116	118	120	120	121	122	123	123	124	124	125	126	127	127	128	129	130	133	134	136	136	–	–	136	–	**u oo** DUCK AND WOODPECKER
LONG VOWEL **ae**	137	138	139	140	141	142	143	144	144	145	145	146	146	147	147	148	148	149	151	151	151	152	–	–	152	–	**ae** BABY SNAIL
LONG VOWEL **ee**	153	154	155	156	157	158	159	160	161	162	162	163	164	165	165	166	167	167	169	172	–	173	174	–	175	175	**ee** BREEDING EAGLE
LONG VOWEL **ie**	176	177	178	178	180	181	182	182	183	184	184	185	186	187	187	188	189	190	192	–	–	193	193	194	–	194	**ie** LIVELY LION
LONG VOWEL **oe**	195	195	196	197	197	198	199	200	200	201	201	201	202	202	203	204	206	206	207	208	208	208	209	–	209	209	**oe** LONELY GOAT
LONG VOWELS **ue oo**	210	211	212	213	213	214	214	215	215	216	216	216	217	218	218	219	219	220	221	222	223	223	223	–	224	224	**ue oo** SMOOTH NEWT

Lesson 3

Aims: The student should be able to:

a) identify long vowel sounds, in the third part of the Dictionary, in a selection of words

b) use the Index to find the page numbers for a selection of words

c) look up words in all three parts of the Dictionary.

1 Begin with listening and speaking activities, starting with the animal names from the third part of the Dictionary: **shark**, **bear**, **bird**, **horse**, **oyster** and **owl**.

Ask the students if they can hear certain vowel sounds in each of these animal names, for example, 'Can you hear /**ar**/ in **shark**?', 'Can you hear /**or**/ in **owl**?'.

Make the vowel sounds longer and louder if you need to.

Continue until responses are confident and correct and then move on to identifying these long vowel sounds in other words. For example, 'Can you hear /**ar**/ in **harmless**?', 'Can you hear /**oi**/ in **early**?'.

Again, continue until the responses are confident and correct.

Selecting one of these long vowel sounds, ask students if they can hear the sound in a variety of words. For example, 'Can you hear /**ar**/ in **car**, **fir**, **jar**, **tar**?'.

Finally, ask students to give you the vowel sound they can hear in the third group of vowel animal names, giving a choice of three. For example, 'What is the vowel sound in **shark**: /**ar**/, /**ae**/ or /**or**/?'. Continue with the different animals and three vowel sound choices until the sounds in all the third group of vowel animal names are correctly identified.

2 Practise using the Index to find page numbers for words containing the sounds /**ar**/, /**air**/, /**er**/, /**or**/, /**oi**/ and /**ou**/. Each student should have a copy of the whole Index (see Index 3 on page 11). Teachers may also like to make a digital copy for class tuition.

Beginning with the animal picture words, ask students first to point to the shark picture next to the letters 'ar', which stand for the sound /**ar**/. Ask which letter **shark** begins with and ask them to point to the letter 'S' in the alphabet across the top of the page. Then, show them how to move one finger along the line of page numbers from /**ar**/ and the other finger down from 'S', until they meet at a page number. **Shark** is on page 234!

Repeat this exercise with **rare**, **worm**, **warlike**, **oyster** and **sound**.

You may need to prompt students with the vowel sound initially, but continue the exercise until the page numbers can be found by the students themselves.

Once students can readily achieve this, ask them to find the page numbers for the following animal words: **armadillo**, **cow**, **earthworm**, **gerbil**, **hound**, **mouse**, **partridge**, **sardine**, **starfish**, **tortoise**.

This time they will need to identify the spelling picture for the vowel sound first. For example, what is the first vowel sound in **partridge**? It is /**ar**/, which is the same as in **shark**.

Introducing ACE

Use these topic lists until students have mastered using Index 3 to find page numbers.

> burger, cornflakes, flour, lard, marmalade, oil, pork, prawn, sardine, trout
>
> garlic, herbs, parsley, parsnips, pear, soya, sprouts, strawberry, turnip, walnut
>
> boiler, carton, door, fork, jar, larder, margarine, starch, torch, towel

After working with Index 3, ask students to find the page numbers for words from any of the three parts, using the following lists. If there is any confusion between any pair of patterns, ask, for example, 'Is it /a/ or /ow/?', 'Is it /o/ or /ar/?' as appropriate.

> aquamarine, brown, cream, ginger, grey, lilac, orange, pink, purple, rose, scarlet, silver, turquoise, violet, yellow
>
> blouse, braces, coat, jacket, leggings, overalls, sandals, scarf, shorts, skirt, slippers, socks, tights, trainers, trousers
>
> brushing, counting, cutting, ironing, learning, marking, painting, reading, serving, sewing, shaving, shopping, sweeping, swimming, working
>
> actor, artist, dentist, diver, doctor, fisherman, hairdresser, joiner, journalist, musician, nurse, plumber, priest, tailor, warden

4 Practise looking up words from the above lists or elsewhere in the dictionary. Note that in some cases (actor, aquamarine, cutting, slippers, sweeping, swimming) the target word is in a section which continues for two or more pages.

Index 3

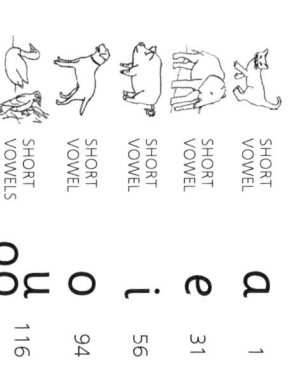

SHORT VOWEL	a	A	B	C	D	E	F	G	H	I	J	K	L	M	N	O	P	Q	R	S	T	U	V	W	X	Y Z
SHORT VOWEL	a	1	5	7	10	11	12	14	16	17	18	18	19	20	21	—	22	24	24	25	28	29	29	30	—	30 30
SHORT VOWEL	e	31	32	33	34	36	39	39	40	41	42	42	43	44	45	45	46	47	48	50	52	53	53	54	54	55 55
SHORT VOWEL	i	56	57	59	61	65	68	70	71	72	77	78	79	80	81	81	82	83	84	87	90	91	91	92	—	— 93
SHORT VOWEL	o	94	95	96	99	99	100	101	102	102	103	103	104	105	105	106	108	109	110	111	113	113	114	114	—	115 115
SHORT VOWELS	u	116	116	118	120	120	121	122	123	123	124	124	125	126	127	127	128	128	129	130	133	134	136	136	—	136 —
LONG VOWEL	oo	210	211	212	213	213	214	214	215	215	216	216	216	217	218	218	219	219	220	221	222	223	223	223	—	224 224
LONG VOWEL	ue	195	195	196	197	197	198	199	200	200	201	201	201	202	202	203	204	206	206	207	208	208	208	209	—	209 209
LONG VOWEL	oe	176	177	178	178	180	181	182	182	183	184	184	185	186	187	187	188	189	189	190	192	—	193	193	194	— 194
LONG VOWEL	ie	153	154	155	156	157	158	159	160	161	162	162	163	164	165	165	166	167	167	169	172	—	—	173	174	— 175
LONG VOWELS	ee	137	138	139	140	141	142	143	144	144	145	145	145	146	146	147	147	148	148	149	151	151	151	151	152	152 175
LONG VOWEL	ae				A	B	C	D	E	F	G	H	I	J	K	L	M	N	O	P	Q	R	S	T	U	V	W X Y Z
VOWEL SOUND	ar	225	226	227	228	228	229	229	230	230	230	231	231	232	232	—	233	233	233	234	235	—	235	—	235	— 235
VOWEL SOUND	air	236	236	236	237	237	238	238	238	239	—	—	239	239	—	—	239	—	240	240	241	—	241	241	—	— —
VOWEL SOUND	er	242	243	244	245	245	246	246	247	247	248	248	248	249	249	250	251	251	252	253	254	254	—	—	255	— 255
VOWEL SOUND	or	256	257	258	259	259	260	261	261	262	262	262	263	263	264	265	266	266	267	268	268	268	269	—	—	269 —
VOWEL SOUND	oi	270	270	270	271	271	272	272	—	—	—	273	273	273	274	274	274	275	275	—	—	275	—	—	—	— —
VOWEL SOUND	ou	276	276	277	278	278	279	279	279	—	280	280	280	281	281	282	283	283	—	—	284	—	284	284	—	— —

a	ACTIVE CAT
e	HEALTHY ELEPHANT
i	BIG PIGLET
o	WATCHFUL DOG
u	
oo	DUCK AND WOODPECKER
ae	BABY SNAIL
ee	BREEDING EAGLE
ie	LIVELY LION
oe	LONELY GOAT
ue	SMOOTH NEWT
ar	BASKING SHARK
air	RARE BEAR
er	EARLY BIRD WITH WORM
or	WARLIKE HORSE
oi	JOYFUL OYSTER
ou	AN OWL SOUND

© David Moseley and Gwyn Singleton 2015 | *ACE Spelling Activities* | LDA | Permission to photocopy

Further activities

Students will now be able to check and correct the spelling of any word they want to use. While most of the checking will be done after a draft has been produced, there should be no absolute ban on using the *ACE Spelling Dictionary* in the course of writing, especially in collaborative work.

As the students are able to look up words for themselves, the teacher should stop supplying spellings on demand. After completing a piece of writing or dictation the students should mark the words they wish to look up (perhaps to a maximum fixed by the teacher). This will not only encourage students' independence, but will also save the teacher time!

The more the Dictionary is used in different subject areas, the greater the benefits will be. Whenever the teacher wants to draw new vocabulary to the attention of the group or class, the students can look up the words in the *ACE Spelling Dictionary* and write them up for display. Homework assignments present further opportunities for Dictionary work.

Initially, it is a good idea to set speed targets for looking up words in the Dictionary. This may be done either as a class or as a homework activity. The words may be taken from prepared lists or may be chosen by the students. If small groups work together, perhaps in competition, they will soon discover good ways of cutting down word-search time and will reach and even exceed the target of 20 seconds per word. This is a realistic target for the words provided in Lessons 1–3, since these do not include words which begin with a neutral vowel sound.

After mastering the basic skill of word-finding by vowel sound and first letter, students will be ready to benefit from further instruction. The section on neutral vowels, on page x of the Dictionary, should form the basis of a separate lesson. Homonyms, plurals and tenses (pages 290–1 of the Dictionary) are also important topics to cover and to return to from time to time.

The *ACE Spelling Dictionary* provides a conceptual framework for understanding the complex relationships between sounds and spellings in English. Word study with the Dictionary, led by the need to communicate and to understand more about written language, is much more than a set of phonic exercises. We provide some starting points in these activity sheets and hope that many more ideas for actively exploring the *ACE Spelling Dictionary* will be developed by teachers and their students.

More word-finding practice
with the ACE Index and Dictionary

Aims: The student should be able to:

1) using the full ACE Index sheet, find and write down the page numbers for 20 specified words in five minutes

2) using the *ACE Spelling Dictionary*, find and write down 20 specified words in ten minutes.

These exercises provide extra practice with the ACE Index after Lessons 1–3 in 'Learning how to use the *ACE Spelling Dictionary*'. Alternatively, they can be used with the Dictionary itself to build up speed in finding words.

The teacher can work with a group or whole class using copies of the Index. The answers can be found at the back of the book.

For one-to-one or small group work, a partner or teaching assistant is needed to read out the words and to check the responses. Alternatively, the exercises can be recorded. If the topic lists are used for looking up words in the Dictionary, each student or small group will need access to a copy.

Introducing ACE

Practice with long vowel sounds

/ae/   /ee/   /ie/   /oe/   /ue/ / /oo/

List of topic words to be read out or played back.

FOOD

1. toast	6. pastry	11. sweet	16. cream
2. ice-cream	7. savoury	12. rice	17. loaf
3. roll	8. muesli	13. oats	18. fruit
4. flavour	9. gravy	14. soup	19. plaice
5. cake	10. meat	15. cheese	20. tasty

IN THE COUNTRY

1. lake	6. stream	11. pool	16. drainage
2. field	7. wheat	12. rye	17. hay
3. acorn	8. oak	13. tree	18. leaves
4. root	9. toadstool	14. flies	19. spider
5. stone	10. bluebells	15. nightingale	20. snake

SPORT

1. team	6. crew	11. race	16. skiing
2. skating	7. rowing	12. climbing	17. glider
3. height	8. diving	13. player	18. bowler
4. fielder	9. boot	14. try	19. goal
5. snooker	10. rival	15. losing	20. rules

OCCUPATIONS

1. playwright	6. director	11. agent	16. poet
2. waiter	7. cleaner	12. labourer	17. dealer
3. salesman	8. librarian	13. student	18. jeweller
4. miner	9. programmer	14. newsagent	19. painter
5. preacher	10. fireman	15. pirate	20. leader

TRAVEL

1. railway	6. road	11. pony	16. plane
2. scooter	7. bicycle	12. flight	17. cruise
3. breakdown	8. timetable	13. train	18. driver
4. motorist	9. wheels	14. pilot	19. vehicle
5. ocean	10. route	15. detour	20. scenery

The student EITHER fills in the page numbers on the sheet OR looks up the words in the *ACE Spelling Dictionary*.

Introducing ACE

Practice with short vowel sounds

/a/ /e/ /i/ /o/ /u/ **/** /oo/

List of topic words to be read out or played back.

WILDLIFE

1. butterfly	6. vixen	11. winkle	16. thrush
2. moth	7. cub	12. cockle	17. dove
3. squirrel	8. otter	13. mussel	18. swan
4. badger	9. jellyfish	14. lobster	19. kestrel
5. fox	10. crab	15. sparrow	20. slug

HOSPITAL

1. ambulance	6. splint	11. health	16. drug
2. bandage	7. temperature	12. lung	17. tablet
3. injury	8. blood	13. oxygen	18. pill
4. fracture	9. vaccine	14. scalpel	19. medication
5. limb	10. stethoscope	15. unconscious	20. stomach

WINTER

1. frost	6. gloves	11. decorate	16. mistletoe
2. shiver	7. anorak	12. presents	17. berries
3. wintry	8. robin	13. tinsel	18. sledge
4. blizzard	9. Christmas	14. glisten	19. pantomime
5. slush	10. carolling	15. holly	20. January

HOLIDAYS

1. sand	6. suntan	11. tent	16. visit
2. bucket	7. cottage	12. caravan	17. exhibition
3. paddle	8. fishing	13. disco	18. restaurant
4. swimming	9. camping	14. shopping	19. customs
5. deckchair	10. rucksack	15. trip	20. luggage

GAMES AND PASTIMES

1. cricket	6. badminton	11. snap	16. rugby
2. chess	7. squash	12. dominoes	17. boxing
3. golf	8. netball	13. lotto	18. sledging
4. hockey	9. putting	14. skipping	19. stilts
5. tennis	10. jigsaws	15. football	20. juggling

The student EITHER fills in the page numbers on the sheet OR looks up the words in the *ACE Spelling Dictionary*.

Introducing ACE

Practice with mixed long and short vowel sounds 1

List of topic words to be read out or played back.

SCHOOL

1. cloakroom	6. lesson	11. lunch	16. copy
2. desk	7. bell	12. monitor	17. science
3. seat	8. break	13. prefect	18. mathematics
4. teacher	9. snack	14. writing	19. games
5. subject	10. queue	15. notes	20. music

DRINKS

1. smoothie	6. chocolate	11. shandy	16. brandy
2. lemonade	7. grapefruit	12. beer	17. alcoholic
3. milk	8. juice	13. cider	18. fizzy
4. coffee	9. wine	14. scotch	19. tonic
5. tea	10. punch	15. whisky	20. soda

GUY FAWKES

1. evening	6. sticks	11. heat	16. banger
2. clothes	7. matches	12. bake	17. fuse
3. fire	8. light	13. sausages	18. taper
4. wood	9. flame	14. fireworks	19. glow
5. paper	10. crackle	15. colours	20. embers

MOUNTAINS

1. peak	6. huge	11. precipice	16. crag
2. massive	7. summit	12. sheer	17. crevice
3. rugged	8. ridge	13. edge	18. trail
4. boulders	9. slope	14. torrent	19. scramble
5. pinnacle	10. avalanche	15. rocky	20. gully

THE RAILWAY STATION

1. ticket	6. platform	11. diesel	16. sleeper
2. office	7. notice	12. carriage	17. signal
3. clock	8. timetable	13. train	18. buffers
4. case	9. kiosk	14. rails	19. bridge
5. trolley	10. engine	15. whistle	20. taxi

The student EITHER **fills in the page numbers on the sheet** OR **looks up the words in the *ACE Spelling Dictionary*.**

Introducing ACE

Practice with mixed long and short vowel sounds 2

List of topic words to be read out or played back.

FUN

1. smile	6. skipping	11. acting	16. chuckling
2. party	7. kissing	12. painting	17. giggling
3. happy	8. hugging	13. joke	18. merry
4. mirth	9. clown	14. tease	19. cartoon
5. joyful	10. tumbling	15. tickle	20. comic

ON THE FARM

1. tractor	6. yard	11. corn	16. cattle
2. plough	7. orchard	12. barley	17. bullock
3. furrow	8. hedgerow	13. crop	18. sheep
4. fertiliser	9. harvest	14. dairy	19. goose
5. slurry	10. grain	15. herd	20. turkey

WATER

1. waves	6. calm	11. whirlpool	16. trickle
2. splash	7. smooth	12. current	17. pour
3. spray	8. tranquil	13. squirt	18. still
4. choppy	9. river	14. jet	19. sparkling
5. rough	10. flow	15. fountain	20. pure

FLOWERS

1. snowdrop	6. tulip	11. lily	16. foxglove
2. cowslip	7. marigold	12. lavender	17. thistle
3. hyacinth	8. pansy	13. heather	18. poppy
4. crocus	9. carnation	14. gorse	19. buttercup
5. daffodil	10. orchid	15. broom	20. daisy

TREES

1. chestnut	6. birch	11. fir	16. oak
2. beech	7. ash	12. pine	17. olive
3. willow	8. palm	13. spruce	18. hazel
4. sycamore	9. holly	14. yew	19. mulberry
5. poplar	10. larch	15. bay	20. maple

The student EITHER fills in the page numbers on the sheet OR looks up the words in the *ACE Spelling Dictionary*.

Using ACE

Spellings for sounds

The short /a/ sound as in ACTIVE CAT

Spelt 'a'

Can you work out these words from the clues given? Each word contains the /a/ sound. The stars tell you how many syllables are in the word.

If you like, you can use the *ACE Spelling Dictionary* to help you find the answers.

Check all the spellings, unless you are absolutely sure. When you have filled in the missing letters, write the whole word on the line.

If you are working with a partner, one of you can find the answers while the other writes them down.

	CLUES	SYLLABLES		WRITE
	e.g. good-looking	**	h _ _ _ _ _ _ _	*handsome*
	1. shaft to connect wheels	**	ax _ _	
H	2. forbidden	*	b _ _ _ _ _	
	3. animal of the desert	**	c _ m _ _	
	4. a root vegetable	**	c _ r _ _ _ _	
	5. a section of a book	**	c _ _ _ _ t _ _ _	
	6. to become bigger	**	e _ p _ _ _ _	
	7. easily broken	**	f _ _ g _ _ _	
	8. a damaging chance event	***	ac _ _ d _ _ _ _	
H	9. to take risks	**	g _ _ b _ _	
	10. a suspended bed	**	h _ m _ _ _ _	
	11. spoken in one or more countries	**	l _ _ g _ _ _ _	
H	12. method or way	**	m _ n _ _ _ _	
	13. having a wife or husband	**	m _ r _ _ _ _ _	
H	14. a large Chinese animal	**	p _ _ d _	
	15. a slight wound	*	s _ _ _ _ _	

18

Using ACE

H beside a word means that it is a homonym. A homonym is a word which sounds the same as or very similar to another word, but which has a different meaning. Can you find all the homonyms (or sound-alike words) from the list you have been working on?

Use the *ACE Spelling Dictionary* to find the homonyms you need. Remember, homonyms are marked with a star in the Dictionary and members of a pair or small group are usually quite close to each other.

When you have found all the homonyms, make up a sentence using that word and at least one other homonym: e.g. 'When you buy tin **tacks** you have to pay **tax**'. Write out your sentences below and check the spelling of any hard words in the Dictionary.

Using ACE

Spellings for sounds

The short /e/ sound as in HEALTHY ELEPHANT

Spelt 'ai', 'e', 'ea', 'ei', 'eo', 'ie'

Can you work out these words from the clues given? Each word contains the /e/ sound. The stars tell you how many syllables are in the word.

If you like, you can use the *ACE Spelling Dictionary* to help you find the answers.

Check all the spellings, unless you are absolutely sure. When you have filled in the missing letters, write the whole word on the line.

If you are working with a partner, one of you can find the answers while the other writes them down.

CLUES	SYLLABLES		WRITE
e.g. an animal with spots	**	l _ p _ _ _	*leopard*
1. once more	**	ag _ _ _	
2. a long wooden seat	*	b _ _ _ _	
3. underground storage room	**	c _ l _ _ _	
4. stockist of medicines	**	c _ _ _ i _ _	
5. money owed	*	d _ _ _	
6. way out	**	e _ i _	
7. person known and liked	*	f _ _ _ _	
8. someone who accepts an invitation	*	g _ _ _ _	
9. free time	**	l _ _ s _ _ _	
10. what is learned	**	l _ s _ _ _	
11. grassy field	**	m _ _ _ d _ _	
12. foot lever	**	p _ d _ _	
13. a liquid fuel	**	p _ _ t _ _ _	
14. a safe haven	**	r _ f _ _ _	
15. very fine cord used for sewing	*	t _ _ _ _ _ _	

ⓗ beside a word means that it is a homonym. A homonym is a word which sounds the same as or very similar to another word, but which has a different meaning. Can you find all the homonyms (or sound-alike words) from the list you have been working on?

Use the *ACE Spelling Dictionary* to find the homonyms you need. Remember, homonyms are marked with a star in the Dictionary and members of a pair or small group are usually quite close to each other.

When you have found all the homonyms, make up a sentence using that word and at least one other homonym: e.g. 'The **weather** will change **whether** we like it or not'. Write out your sentences below and check the spelling of any hard words in the Dictionary.

Using ACE

Spellings for sounds

The short /i/ sound as in BIG PIGLET

Spelt 'i', 'u', 'ui', 'y'

Can you work out these words from the clues given? Each word contains the /i/ sound. The stars tell you how many syllables are in the word.

If you like, you can use the *ACE Spelling Dictionary* to help you find the answers.

Check all the spellings, unless you are absolutely sure. When you have filled in the missing letters, write the whole word on the line.

If you are working with a partner, one of you can find the answers while the other writes them down.

	CLUES	SYLLABLES		WRITE
	e.g. to whip with a circular movement	*	w _ _ _ _	*whisk*
	1. way over a river	*	b _ _ _ _ _	
ⓗ	2. to construct	*	b _ _ _ _	
	3. December 25th	**	C _ _ _ _ m _ _	
	4. like clear glass	**	c _ _ s _ _ _ _	
	5. very dirty	**	f _ _ t _ _	
ⓗ	6. a song sung in church	*	h _ _ _	
	7. a room in which food is cooked	**	k _ t _ _ _ _	
	8. neither solid nor gas	**	l _ q _ _ _	
	9. 60 seconds	**	m _ n _ _ _	
	10. small handgun	**	p _ _ t _ _	
	11. active and hardworking	**	b _ _ _ _	
ⓗ	12. jewellery worn on a finger	*	r _ _ _ _	
ⓗ	13. signs which have meaning	**	s _ _ b _ _ _	
ⓗ	14. a wicked person	**	v _ l _ _ _ _	
ⓗ	15. a woman thought to use magic	*	w _ _ _ _	

Using ACE

H beside a word means that it is a homonym. A homonym is a word which sounds the same as or very similar to another word, but which has a different meaning. Can you find all the homonyms (or sound-alike words) from the list you have been working on?

Use the *ACE Spelling Dictionary* to find the homonyms you need. Remember, homonyms are marked with a star in the Dictionary and members of a pair or small group are usually quite close to each other.

When you have found all the homonyms, make up a sentence using that word and at least one other homonym: e.g. 'The **prince** has a large collection of old **prints**'. Write out your sentences below and check the spelling of any hard words in the Dictionary.

Using ACE

Spellings for sounds

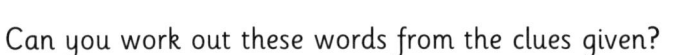

The short /o/ sound as in WATCHFUL DOG

Spelt 'a', 'o'

Can you work out these words from the clues given?
Each word contains the /o/ sound. The stars tell you how many syllables are in the word.

If you like, you can use the *ACE Spelling Dictionary* to help you find the answers.

Check all the spellings, unless you are absolutely sure. When you have filled in the missing letters, write the whole word on the line.

If you are working with a partner, one of you can find the answers while the other writes them down.

	CLUES	SYLLABLES		WRITE
	e.g. a citrus fruit	**	or _ _ _ _	*orange*
	1. an explosive device	*	b _ _ _	
H	2. to defeat in war	**	c _ _ q _ _ _	
	3. an intelligent sea mammal	**	d _ _ p _ _ _	
	4. shiny	**	g _ _ _ _ y	
	5. banged	*	k _ _ _ _ _	
H	6. a tied fastening	*	k _ _ _	
	7. a shellfish with big claws	**	l _ _ s _ _ _	
	8. a place of worship for Muslims	*	m _ _ _ _ _	
	9. a book containing a long story	**	n _ v _ _	
	10. a fruit which yields oil	**	ol _ _ _ _	
	11. eggs beaten and fried	**	o _ _ l _ _ _ _	
H	12. financial gain	**	p _ _ f _ _	
	13. a place where rocks are blasted	**	q _ _ r _	
	14. to squeeze tightly	*	s _ _ _ _ _	
H	15. unit of electric power	*	w _ _ _	

Ⓗ beside a word means that it is a homonym. A homonym is a word which sounds the same as or very similar to another word, but which has a different meaning. Can you find all the homonyms (or sound-alike words) from the list you have been working on?

Use the *ACE Spelling Dictionary* to find the homonyms you need. Remember, homonyms are marked with a star in the Dictionary and members of a pair or small group are usually quite close to each other.

When you have found all the homonyms, make up a sentence using that word and at least one other homonym: e.g. 'The **cops** hid among the trees in the **copse**'. Write out your sentences below and check the spelling of any hard words in the Dictionary.

Using ACE

Spellings for sounds

The short /u/ or /oo/ sound as in DUCK AND WOODPECKER
Spelt 'o', 'o–e', 'ou', 'u'

Can you work out these words from the clues given? Each word contains the /u/ or /oo/ sound. The stars tell you how many syllables are in the word.

If you like, you can use the *ACE Spelling Dictionary* to help you find the answers.

Check all the spellings, unless you are absolutely sure. When you have filled in the missing letters, write the whole word on the line.

If you are working with a partner, one of you can find the answers while the other writes them down.

	CLUES	SYLLABLES		WRITE
	e.g. very ripe and delicious	**	l _ s _ _ _ _	*luscious*
1.	in the middle of	**	am _ _ _	
2.	to go red with embarrassment	*	b _ _ _ _	
3.	steamed or cooked dish, often sweet	**	p _ dd _ _	
4.	dried fruit, used in cakes	**	c _ r _ _ _ _	
5.	sufficient	**	en _ _ _ _	
6.	worn on the hands	*	g _ _ _ _ _	
7.	a baby buggy	**	p _ _ _ ch _ _	
8.	wild animals that hunt in packs	*	w _ l _ _ s	
9.	a soft, purple fruit	*	p _ _ _	
10.	a woman living in a convent	*	n _ _	
11.	stuff to be thrown away	**	r _ b _ _ _ _	
12.	bones protecting the brain	*	s _ _ _ _	
13.	at least a small amount or number	*	s _ _ _	
14.	unwanted problems	**	t _ _ _ b _ _ _	
15.	to the floor above	**	u _ s _ _ _ _ _	

H beside a word means that it is a homonym. A homonym is a word which sounds the same as or very similar to another word, but which has a different meaning. Can you find all the homonyms (or sound-alike words) from the list you have been working on?

Use the *ACE Spelling Dictionary* to find the homonyms you need. Remember, homonyms are marked with a star in the Dictionary and members of a pair or small group are usually quite close to each other.

When you have found all the homonyms, make up a sentence using that word and at least one other homonym: e.g. 'She was the **one** who **won** a holiday'. Write out your sentences below and check the spelling of any hard words in the Dictionary.

Using ACE

Spellings for sounds

The short /**ae**/ sound as in BABY SNAIL

Spelt 'a', 'a–e', 'ai', 'ay', 'ea', 'ei'

Can you work out these words from the clues given? Each word contains the /**ae**/ sound. The stars tell you how many syllables are in the word.

If you like, you can use the *ACE Spelling Dictionary* to help you find the answers.

Check all the spellings, unless you are absolutely sure. When you have filled in the missing letters, write the whole word on the line.

If you are working with a partner, one of you can find the answers while the other writes them down.

	CLUES	SYLLABLES		WRITE
	e.g. a flatfish	*	p _ _ _ _ _	*plaice*
	1. a continuing pain	*	a _ _ _	
	2. very old indeed	**	a _ c _ _ _ _	
H	3. to smash into pieces	*	b _ _ _ _	
	4. a baby's bed	**	c _ _ d _ _	
	5. to breathe out	**	e _ h _ _ _	
	6. well-known	**	f _ m _ _ _	
H	7. a way of walking	*	g _ _ _	
H	8. rub into small pieces	*	g _ _ _ _	
	9. misty	**	h _ _ _	
	10. prison	*	j _ _ _	
	11. put down in one place	*	l _ _ _	
H	12. letters and parcels	*	m _ _ _	
	13. an error	**	m _ _ t _ _ _	
H	14. a board for carrying things	*	t _ _ _	
H	15. heaviness	*	w _ _ _ _ _	

28 © David Moseley and Gwyn Singleton 2015 | *ACE Spelling Activities* | LDA | Permission to photocopy

H beside a word means that it is a homonym. A homonym is a word which sounds the same as or very similar to another word, but which has a different meaning. Can you find all the homonyms (or sound-alike words) from the list you have been working on?

Use the *ACE Spelling Dictionary* to find the homonyms you need. Remember, homonyms are marked with a star in the Dictionary and members of a pair or small group are usually quite close to each other.

When you have found all the homonyms, make up a sentence using that word and at least one other homonym: e.g. 'Will **plaice** do in **place** of cod?'. Write out your sentences below and check the spelling of any hard words in the Dictionary.

Using ACE

Spellings for sounds

The sound /ee/ as in BREEDING EAGLE

Spelt 'e', 'ea', 'ee', 'ei', 'ey'

Can you work out these words from the clues given? Each word contains the /ee/ sound. The stars tell you how many syllables are in the word.

If you like, you can use the *ACE Spelling Dictionary* to help you find the answers.

Check all the spellings, unless you are absolutely sure. When you have filled in the missing letters, write the whole word on the line.

If you are working with a partner, one of you can find the answers while the other writes them down.

	CLUES	SYLLABLES		WRITE
	e.g. trousers made of denim	*	j _ _ _ _	*jeans*
	1. to come into view	**	ap _ _ _ _	
	2. hard-backed insect	**	b _ _ t _ _	
(H)	3. a squeaking noise	*	c _ _ _ _	
(H)	4. an animal found in forests	*	d _ _ _	
	5. to mislead with lies	**	d _ c _ _ _ _	
	6. keen and enthusiastic	**	e _ g _ _	
	7. having the same value	**	eq _ _ _ _	
	8. occurring often	**	f _ _ q _ _ _ _	
	9. opening in a lock	**	k _ _ h _ _ _	
(H)	10. rented	*	l _ _ _ _	
(H)	11. measuring machine	**	m _ t _ _	
	12. small tool used for sewing	**	n _ _ d _ _	
(H)	13. period without war	*	p _ _ _ _	
	14. feeling sick	**	q _ _ _ s _	
	15. grab hold of	*	s _ _ _ _	

30

Ⓗ beside a word means that it is a homonym. A homonym is a word which sounds the same as or very similar to another word, but which has a different meaning. Can you find all the homonyms (or sound-alike words) from the list you have been working on?

Use the *ACE Spelling Dictionary* to find the homonyms you need. Remember, homonyms are marked with a star in the Dictionary and members of a pair or small group are usually quite close to each other.

When you have found all the homonyms, make up a sentence using that word and at least one other homonym: e.g. 'It is not easy to **steal** a safe made of **steel**'. Write out your sentences below and check the spelling of any hard words in the Dictionary.

Using ACE

Spellings for sounds

The sound /ie/ as in LIVELY LION

Spelt 'i', 'i–e', 'igh', 'uy', 'y', 'ye'

Can you work out these words from the clues given? Each word contains the /ie/ sound. The stars tell you how many syllables are in the word.

If you like, you can use the *ACE Spelling Dictionary* to help you find the answers.

Check all the spellings, unless you are absolutely sure. When you have filled in the missing letters, write the whole word on the line.

If you are working with a partner, one of you can find the answers while the other writes them down.

	CLUES	SYLLABLES		WRITE
	e.g. an absence of sound	**	s _ l _ _ _ _	*silence*
	1. muscles in the arm	**	b _ c _ _ _ _	
ⓗ	2. gear for handling a horse	**	b _ _ d _ _	
ⓗ	3. someone who makes a purchase	**	b _ y _ _	
	4. a person riding a bicycle	**	c _ c _ _ _ _	
	5. to weaken a solution	**	d _ l _ _ _	
ⓗ	6. coloured liquid for staining	*	d _ _	
	7. to ask	**	e _ q _ _ _	
	8. good advice	**	g _ _ d _ _ _ _	
ⓗ	9. an image that is worshipped	**	id _ _	
ⓗ	10. an electric flash in the sky	**	l _ _ _ _ n _ _ _	
ⓗ	11. may, perhaps	*	m _ _ _ _	
	12. tall metal support for cables	**	p _ l _ _	
	13. rise and fall of the sea	*	t _ d _	
ⓗ	14. make weary	*	t _ _ _ _	
	15. to shake rapidly	**	v _ b _ _ _ _	

H beside a word means that it is a homonym. A homonym is a word which sounds the same as or very similar to another word, but which has a different meaning. Can you find all the homonyms (or sound-alike words) from the list you have been working on?

Use the *ACE Spelling Dictionary* to find the homonyms you need. Remember, homonyms are marked with a star in the Dictionary and members of a pair or small group are usually quite close to each other.

When you have found all the homonyms, make up a sentence using that word and at least one other homonym: e.g. 'If the cost is **higher** we won't **hire** it'. Write out your sentences below and check the spelling of any hard words in the Dictionary.

Using ACE

Spellings for sounds

The sound /oe/ as in LONELY GOAT

Spelt 'o', 'oa', 'o–e', 'ough', 'ow'

Can you work out these words from the clues given? Each word contains the /oe/ sound. The stars tell you how many syllables are in the word.

If you like, you can use the *ACE Spelling Dictionary* to help you find the answers.

Check all the spellings, unless you are absolutely sure. When you have filled in the missing letters, write the whole word on the line.

If you are working with a partner, one of you can find the answers while the other writes them down.

	CLUES	SYLLABLES		WRITE
	e.g. comfy and warm	**	c _ s _	cosy
Ⓗ	1. brave and courageous	*	b _ _ _	
	2. a burglar may use this tool	**	c _ _ _ b _ _	
Ⓗ	3. flour and water mixed together	*	d _ _ _ _	
	4. made solid by the cold	**	f _ _ z _ _	
	5. to shine in the dark	*	g _ _ _	
	6. an adult	**	g _ _ _ _ _ -u _	
Ⓗ	7. something lent	*	l _ _ _	
	8. to complain or groan in pain	*	m _ _ _	
	9. an enormous area of sea	**	o _ _ _ _	
	10. to cook gently in water	*	p _ _ _ _	
Ⓗ	11. lines of things	*	r _ _ _	
	12. a white winter flower	**	s _ _ _ d _ _ _	
Ⓗ	13. under-part of the foot	*	s _ _ _	
	14. a monarch's chair	*	t _ _ _ _ _	
Ⓗ	15. the yellow part of an egg	*	y _ _ _	

Using ACE

Ⓗ beside a word means that it is a homonym. A homonym is a word which sounds the same as or very similar to another word, but which has a different meaning. Can you find all the homonyms (or sound-alike words) from the list you have been working on?

Use the *ACE Spelling Dictionary* to find the homonyms you need. Remember, homonyms are marked with a star in the Dictionary and members of a pair or small group are usually quite close to each other.

When you have found all the homonyms, make up a sentence using that word and at least one other homonym: e.g. 'The **whole** class helped to dig the **hole**'. Write out your sentences below and check the spelling of any hard words in the Dictionary.

Using ACE

Spellings for sounds

The sound /ue/ or /oo/ as in SMOOTH NEWT

Spelt 'eau', 'eu', 'ew', 'oo', 'u', 'u–e', 'ui'

Can you work out these words from the clues given? Each word contains the /oo/ or /ue/ sound. The stars tell you how many syllables are in the word.

If you like, you can use the *ACE Spelling Dictionary* to help you find the answers.

Check all the spellings, unless you are absolutely sure. When you have filled in the missing letters, write the whole word on the line.

If you are working with a partner, one of you can find the answers while the other writes them down.

CLUES	SYLLABLES		WRITE
e.g. travel bag for clothes	**	s _ _ _ c _ _ _	*suitcase*
1. to cause laughter or fun	**	am _ _ _ _	
2. great attractiveness	**	b _ _ _ _ _	
3. a dark-coloured injury	*	b _ _ _ _	
4. to select	*	c _ _ _ _ _	
5. to holiday on a boat	*	c _ _ _ _ _	
6. morning wetness on the grass	*	d _ _	
7. a continent	**	E _ _ _ _ _	
8. depressed, cheerless	**	g _ _ _ _ _	
9. the feet of horses or goats	*	h _ _ _ _	
10. a liquid from fruit	*	j _ _ _ _	
11. recently made or obtained	*	n _ _	
12. a pest, something annoying	**	n _ _ s _ _ _ _	
13. to damage with unwanted material	**	p _ ll _ _ _	
14. burial or cremation ceremony	**	f _ _ _ _ _ _	
15. to fire a gun	*	s _ _ _ _	

Ⓗ beside a word means that it is a homonym. A homonym is a word which sounds the same as or very similar to another word, but which has a different meaning. Can you find all the homonyms (or sound-alike words) from the list you have been working on?

Use the *ACE Spelling Dictionary* to find the homonyms you need. Remember, homonyms are marked with a star in the Dictionary and members of a pair or small group are usually quite close to each other.

When you have found all the homonyms, make up a sentence using that word and at least one other homonym: e.g. 'He joined the **queue** for a free snooker **cue**'. Write out your sentences below and check the spelling of any hard words in the Dictionary.

Using ACE

Spellings for sounds

*The sound /**ar**/ as in BASKING SHARK*

Spelt 'a', 'ar', 'arrh', 'ear', 'er'

Can you work out these words from the clues given? Each word contains the /**ar**/ sound. The stars tell you how many syllables are in the word.

If you like, you can use the *ACE Spelling Dictionary* to help you find the answers.

Check all the spellings, unless you are absolutely sure. When you have filled in the missing letters, write the whole word on the line.

If you are working with a partner, one of you can find the answers while the other writes them down.

	CLUES	SYLLABLES		WRITE
	e.g. a good buy	**	b _ _ g _ _ _	*bargain*
ⒽH	1. part of a circle	*	a _ _	
	2. a grain crop	**	b _ _ l _ _	
	3. a floor covering	**	c _ _ p _ _	
	4. a cardboard container	**	c _ _ t _ _	
	5. mucus in the nose and throat	**	c _ t _ _ _	
ⒽH	6. a greater distance	**	f _ _ t _ _ _	
	7. stringed musical instrument	**	g _ _ t _ _	
	8. spear for hunting fish	**	h _ _ p _ _ _	
	9. time to gather in crops	**	h _ _ v _ _	
ⒽH	10. organ that pumps blood	*	h _ _ _ _	
	11. a light beer	**	l _ g _ _	
	12. a packet	**	p _ _ c _ _	
	13. worn round the neck	*	s _ _ _	
	14. rank in the army	**	s _ _ g _ _ _ _	
	15. a clear paint	**	v _ _ n _ _ _	

38

Ⓗ beside a word means that it is a homonym. A homonym is a word which sounds the same as or very similar to another word, but which has a different meaning. Can you find all the homonyms (or sound-alike words) from the list you have been working on?

Use the *ACE Spelling Dictionary* to find the homonyms you need. Remember, homonyms are marked with a star in the Dictionary and members of a pair or small group are usually quite close to each other.

When you have found all the homonyms, make up a sentence using that word and at least one other homonym: e.g. 'We **aren't** going to stay with our **aunt**'. Write out your sentences below and check the spelling of any hard words in the Dictionary.

Using ACE

Spellings for sounds

The sound /air/ as in RARE BEAR

Spelt 'a', 'air', 'are', 'ere'

Can you work out these words from the clues given? Each word contains the /**air**/ sound. The stars tell you how many syllables are in the word.

If you like, you can use the *ACE Spelling Dictionary* to help you find the answers.

Check all the spellings, unless you are absolutely sure. When you have filled in the missing letters, write the whole word on the line.

If you are working with a partner, one of you can find the answers while the other writes them down.

	CLUES	SYLLABLES		WRITE
	e.g. make-believe little folk	**	f _ _ _ _ _	*fairies*
	1. conscious	**	aw _ _ _	
(H)	2. uncovered	*	b _ _ _	
	3. hardly	**	b _ _ _ l _	
	4. lacking attention, not thorough	**	c _ _ l _ _ _ _	
	5. bravely taking risks	**	d _ r _ _ _	
(H)	6. charge for a ride	*	f _ _ _	
	7. goodbye	**	f _ _ _ w _ _ _	
(H)	8. animal like a rabbit	*	h _ _ _	
	9. mother or father	**	p _ r _ _ _	
	10. get ready	**	p _ _ p _ _ _	
	11. mend	**	r _ p _ _ _	
	12. frightening	**	s _ _ r _	
(H)	13. look with a fixed gaze	*	s _ _ _ _	
(H)	14. to or in that place	*	t _ _ _ _	
(H)	15. to or in what place	*	w _ _ _ _	

ⓗ beside a word means that it is a homonym. A homonym is a word which sounds the same as or very similar to another word, but which has a different meaning. Can you find all the homonyms (or sound-alike words) from the list you have been working on?

Use the *ACE Spelling Dictionary* to find the homonyms you need. Remember, homonyms are marked with a star in the Dictionary and members of a pair or small group are usually quite close to each other.

When you have found all the homonyms, make up a sentence using that word and at least one other homonym: e.g. 'The **mayor** rode on a grey **mare**'. Write out your sentences below and check the spelling of any hard words in the Dictionary.

Using ACE

Spellings for sounds

The sound /er/ as in EARLY BIRD WITH WORM

Spelt 'ear', 'er', 'ir', 'ol', 'or', 'our', 'ur'

Can you work out these words from the clues given? Each word contains the **/er/** sound. The stars tell you how many syllables are in the word.

If you like, you can use the *ACE Spelling Dictionary* to help you find the answers.

Check all the spellings, unless you are absolutely sure. When you have filled in the missing letters, write the whole word on the line.

If you are working with a partner, one of you can find the answers while the other writes them down.

	CLUES	SYLLABLES		WRITE
	e.g. easily frightened	**	n __ v __ __ __	*nervous*
	1. ridiculous	**	a __ s __ __ __	
	2. on the look-out	**	al __ __ __	
Ⓗ	3. delivery of a baby	*	b __ __ __ __	
	4. thief who breaks in	**	b __ __ g __ __ __	
Ⓗ	5. army officer	**	c __ __ __ n __ __	
	6. not clean	**	d __ __ t __	
Ⓗ	7. to obtain money from working	*	e __ __ __	
Ⓗ	8. coat of an animal	*	f __ __	
	9. to make a bubbling sound	**	g __ __ g __ __	
	10. a daily record or paper	**	j __ __ __ n __ __	
	11. kill	**	m __ __ d __ __	
	12. speak in a low voice	**	m __ __ m __ __	
	13. scent	**	p __ __ f __ __ __	
	14. to buy	**	p __ __ c __ __ __ __	
Ⓗ	15. the earth	*	w __ __ __ __	

42

Using ACE

Ⓗ beside a word means that it is a homonym. A homonym is a word which sounds the same as or very similar to another word, but which has a different meaning. Can you find all the homonyms (or sound-alike words) from the list you have been working on?

Use the *ACE Spelling Dictionary* to find the homonyms you need. Remember, homonyms are marked with a star in the Dictionary and members of a pair or small group are usually quite close to each other.

When you have found all the homonyms, make up a sentence using that word and at least one other homonym: e.g. 'We took **turns** to look through the binoculars at the **terns**'. Write out your sentences below and check the spelling of any hard words in the Dictionary.

Spellings for sounds

*The sound /**or**/ as in WARLIKE HORSE*

Spelt 'al', 'ar', 'au', 'augh', 'aw', 'oar', 'or', 'ore', 'our'

Can you work out these words from the clues given? Each word contains the /**or**/ sound. The stars tell you how many syllables are in the word.

If you like, you can use the *ACE Spelling Dictionary* to help you find the answers.

Check all the spellings, unless you are absolutely sure. When you have filled in the missing letters, write the whole word on the line.

If you are working with a partner, one of you can find the answers while the other writes them down.

CLUES	SYLLABLES		WRITE
e.g. an animal you ride	*	h _ _ _ _	horse
1. dreadful	**	a _ f _ _ _	
2. a plank	*	b _ _ _ _	
3. a girl child	**	d _ _ _ _ t _ _	
4. strength or power	*	f _ _ _ _	
5. wealth, good luck	**	f _ _ t _ _ _	
6. splendid and attractive	**	g _ _ g _ _ _ _	
7. to visit as a ghost	*	h _ _ _ _ _	
8. a bird of prey	*	h _ _ _ _	
9. a period of grief after loss	**	m _ _ _ _ i _ _	
10. mischievous and disobedient	**	n _ _ _ _ _ t _	
11. cup and —	**	s _ _ c _ _	
12. beach	*	s _ _ _ _	
13. stem	*	s _ _ _ _	
14. to go somewhere on foot	*	w _ _ _	
15. prolonged fighting	*	w _ _	

H beside a word means that it is a homonym. A homonym is a word which sounds the same as or very similar to another word, but which has a different meaning. Can you find all the homonyms (or sound-alike words) from the list you have been working on?

Use the *ACE Spelling Dictionary* to find the homonyms you need. Remember, homonyms are marked with a star in the Dictionary and members of a pair or small group are usually quite close to each other.

When you have found all the homonyms, make up a sentence using that word and at least one other homonym: e.g. 'They **fought** hard to capture the **fort**'. Write out your sentences below and check the spelling of any hard words in the Dictionary.

Using ACE

Spellings for sounds

The sound /oi/ as in JOYFUL OYSTER

Spelt 'oi', 'oy', 'uoy'

Can you work out these words from the clues given? Each word contains the /**oi**/ sound. The stars tell you how many syllables are in the word.

If you like, you can use the *ACE Spelling Dictionary* to help you find the answers.

Check all the spellings, unless you are absolutely sure. When you have filled in the missing letters, write the whole word on the line.

If you are working with a partner, one of you can find the answers while the other writes them down.

CLUES	SYLLABLES		WRITE
e.g. unpleasant loud sound	*	n _ _ _ _	noise
1. keep away from	* *	a _ _ _ _	
2. bubbling hot	* *	b _ _ l _ _ _	
3. floating marker	*	b _ _ _	
4. what you choose	*	c _ _ _ _ _	
5. money	*	c _ _ _	
6. take on for work	* *	e _ p _ _ _	
7. a large entrance hall	* *	f _ _ e _	
8. to heave up	*	h _ _ _ _	
9. full of happiness	* *	j _ _ f _ _	
10. soothing cream	* *	o _ _ _ m _ _ _	
11. shellfish in which pearls grow	* *	o _ s _ _ _	
12. kill with a deadly substance	* *	p _ _ s _ _	
13. show great happiness	* *	r _ j _ _ _	
14. made dirty	*	s _ _ _ _ _	
15. hard work	*	t _ _ _	

46

Ⓗ beside a word means that it is a homonym. A homonym is a word which sounds the same as or very similar to another word, but which has a different meaning. Can you find all the homonyms (or sound-alike words) from the list you have been working on?

Use the *ACE Spelling Dictionary* to find the homonyms you need. Remember, homonyms are marked with a star in the Dictionary and members of a pair or small group are usually quite close to each other.

When you have found all the homonyms, make up a sentence using that word and at least one other homonym: e.g. 'I hurt my **groin** when I tried to leap over the **groyne**'. Write out your sentences below and check the spelling of any hard words in the Dictionary.

Using ACE

Spellings for sounds

The sound /ou/ as in AN OWL SOUND

Spelt 'ou', 'ough', 'ow'

Can you work out these words from the clues given? Each word contains the /**ou**/ sound. The stars tell you how many syllables are in the word.

If you like, you can use the *ACE Spelling Dictionary* to help you find the answers.

Check all the spellings, unless you are absolutely sure. When you have filled in the missing letters, write the whole word on the line.

If you are working with a partner, one of you can find the answers while the other writes them down.

	CLUES	SYLLABLES		WRITE
	e.g. a small animal with a long tail	*	m _ _ _ _	*mouse*
ⓗ	1. permitted	**	all _ _ _ _	
ⓗ	2. a branch	*	b _ _ _ _	
ⓗ	3. a person who lacks courage	**	c _ _ a _ _	
	4. a large group of people	*	c _ _ _ _	
	5. almost falling asleep	**	d _ _ s _	
ⓗ	6. blossom	**	f _ _ _ _ _	
ⓗ	7. disgusting	*	f _ _ _	
ⓗ	8. period of time	*	h _ _ _	
	9. part of the face	*	m _ _ _ _	
	10. dig up into furrows	*	p _ _ _ _	
	11. a game with bat and ball	**	r _ _ _ d _ _ _	
	12. noisy and badly behaved	**	r _ _ _ d _	
	13. start to grow	*	s _ _ _ _ _	
	14. 10 × 100	**	t _ _ _ s _ _ _	
	15. a garden tool	**	t _ _ _ _ _	

48

ⓗ beside a word means that it is a homonym. A homonym is a word which sounds the same as or very similar to another word, but which has a different meaning. Can you find all the homonyms (or sound-alike words) from the list you have been working on?

Use the *ACE Spelling Dictionary* to find the homonyms you need. Remember, homonyms are marked with a star in the Dictionary and members of a pair or small group are usually quite close to each other.

When you have found all the homonyms, make up a sentence using that word and at least one other homonym: e.g. 'I advise and **counsel** you to stand for the **council**'. Write out your sentences below and check the spelling of any hard words in the Dictionary.

Using ACE

Spellings for sounds puzzles

The sound /ae/ as in BABY SNAIL

Can you follow the lines below to join the beginnings and endings of the words to the middle sound /ae/?

Remember that the sound /ae/ will be spelt in different ways, so check the words in the *ACE Spelling Dictionary* before you write them down.

When you have found all seven words, you can use them to fill in the crossword puzzle.

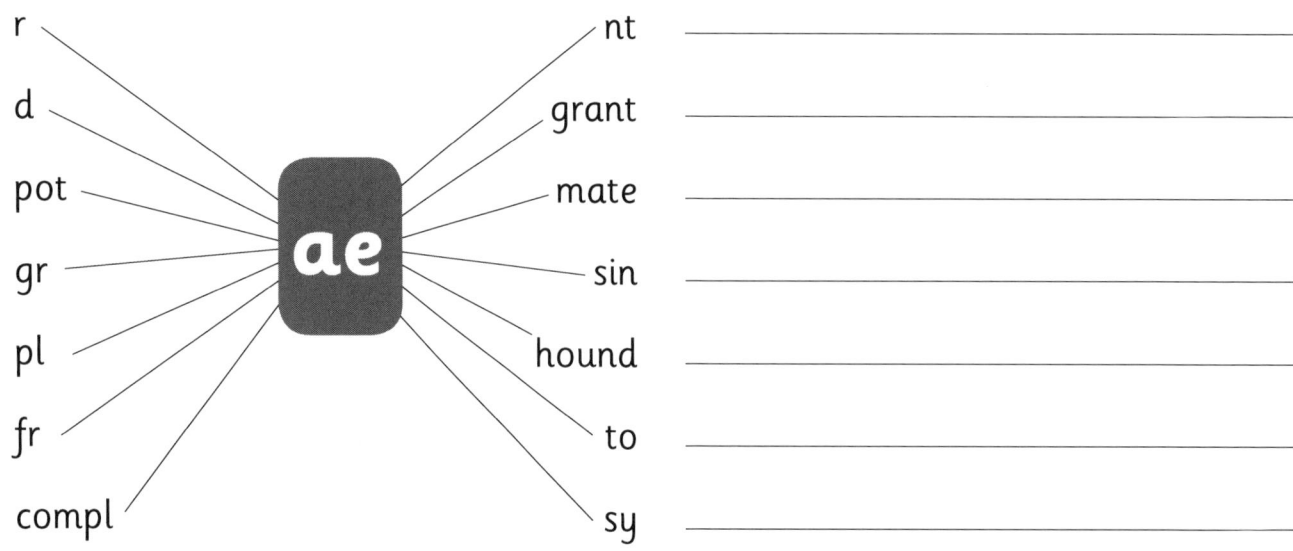

CLUES

1. a vegetable grown in the ground
2. a criticism
3. sweet-smelling
4. a racing dog
5. a common flower
6. a dried grape
7. a friend to have fun with

50

Spellings for sounds puzzles

The sound /ee/ as in BREEDING EAGLE

Can you follow the lines below to join the beginnings and endings of the words to the middle sound /**ee**/?

Remember that the sound /**ee**/ will be spelt in different ways, so check the words in the *ACE Spelling Dictionary* before you write them down.

When you have found all seven words, you can use them to fill in the crossword puzzle.

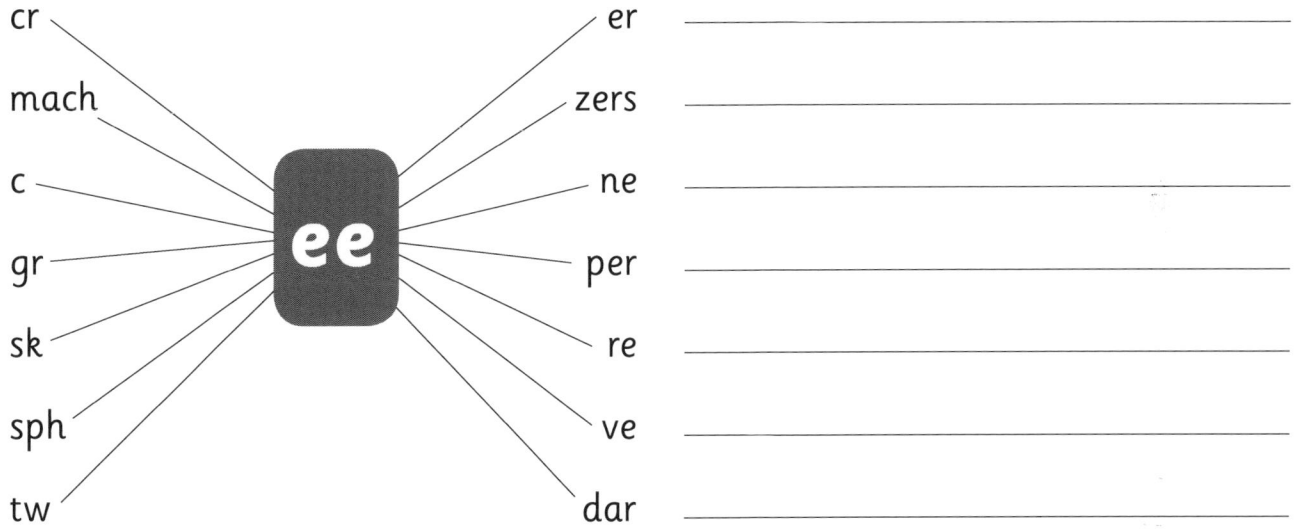

CLUES

1. a person gliding on snow
2. a climbing plant
3. show deep sadness
4. a solid circular shape
5. an evergreen tree
6. an instrument for plucking hairs
7. a mechanical device

Using ACE

Spellings for sounds puzzles

*The sound /**ie**/ as in LIVELY LION*

Can you follow the lines below to join the beginnings and endings of the words to the middle sound /**ie**/?

Remember that the sound /**ie**/ will be spelt in different ways, so check the words in the *ACE Spelling Dictionary* before you write them down.

When you have found all seven words, you can use them to fill in the crossword puzzle.

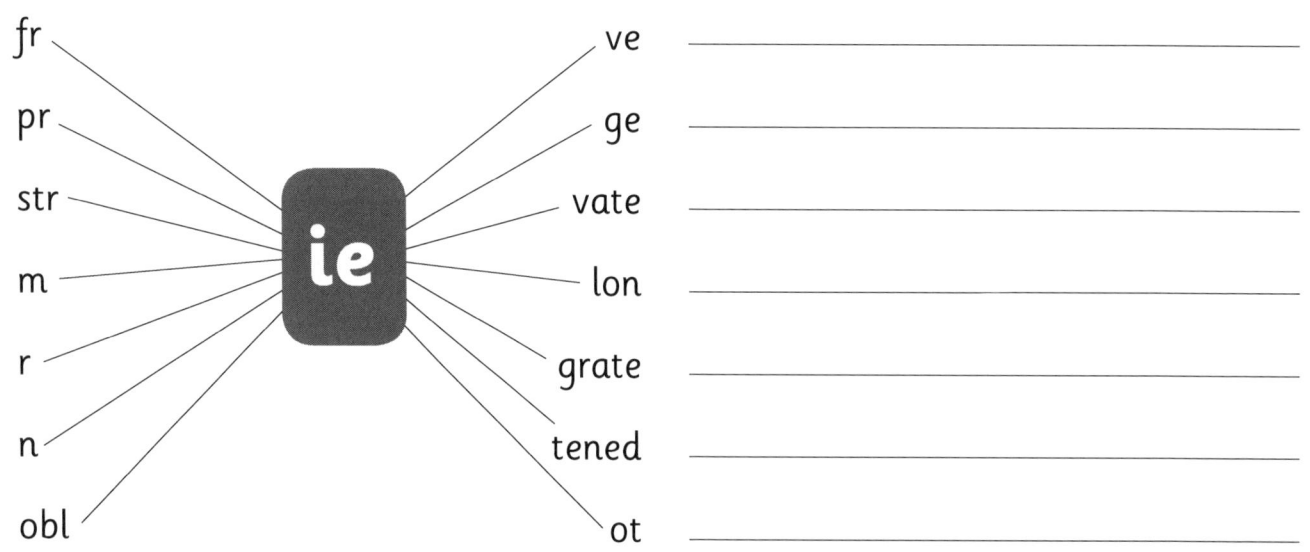

CLUES

1. to work hard to reach an aim

2. a revolt

3. not public

4. afraid

5. a fabric used for making thin tights

6. go to live in another country

7. to do a favour for someone

Using ACE

Spellings for sounds puzzles

The sound /oe/ as in LONELY GOAT

Can you follow the lines below to join the beginnings and endings of the words to the middle sound /oe/?

Remember that the sound /oe/ will be spelt in different ways, so check the words in the *ACE Spelling Dictionary* before you write them down.

When you have found all seven words, you can use them to fill in the crossword puzzle.

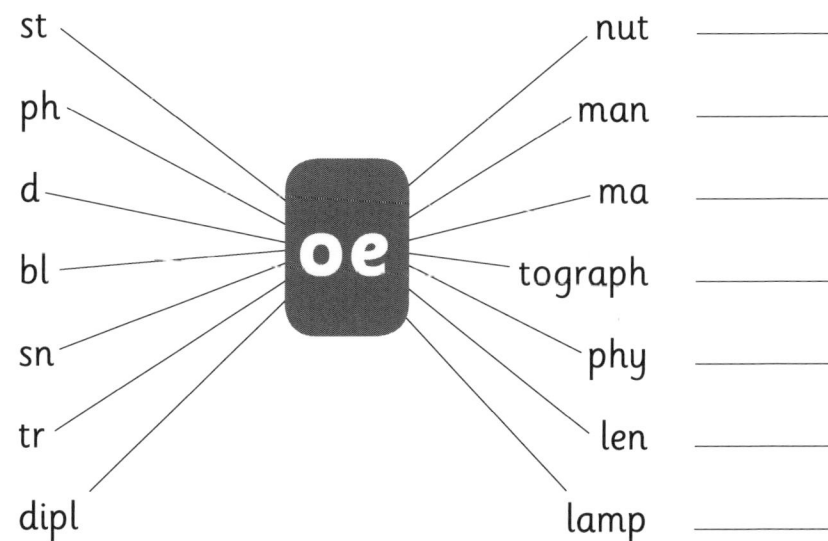

CLUES

1. burner making a hot flame
2. image captured on a camera
3. round cake with a hole
4. prize
5. taken dishonestly
6. figure who melts
7. certificate

Using ACE

Spellings for sounds puzzles

The sounds /oo/ or /ue/ as in SMOOTH NEWT

Can you follow the lines below to join the beginnings and endings of the words to the middle sounds /oo/ or /ue/?

Remember that the sound /oo/ and /ue/ will be spelt in different ways, so check the words in the *ACE Spelling Dictionary* before you write them down.

When you have found all seven words, you can use them to fill in the crossword puzzle.

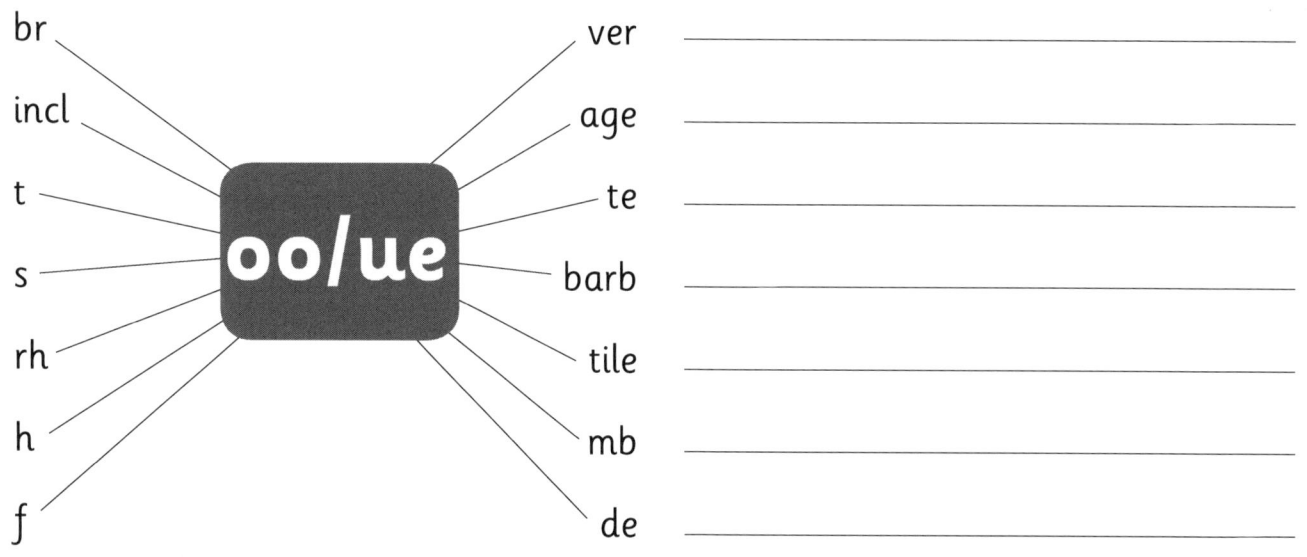

CLUES

1. plant with pink stems, used for pies
2. human waste
3. cleaning machine
4. useless
5. put in a group
6. burial chamber
7. a cruel person

Using ACE

Spellings for sounds puzzles

*The sound /**ar**/ as in BASKING SHARK*

Can you follow the lines below to join the beginnings and endings of the words to the middle sound /**ar**/?

Remember that the sound /**ar**/ will be spelt in different ways, so check the words in the *ACE Spelling Dictionary* before you write them down.

When you have found all seven words, you can use them to fill in the crossword puzzle.

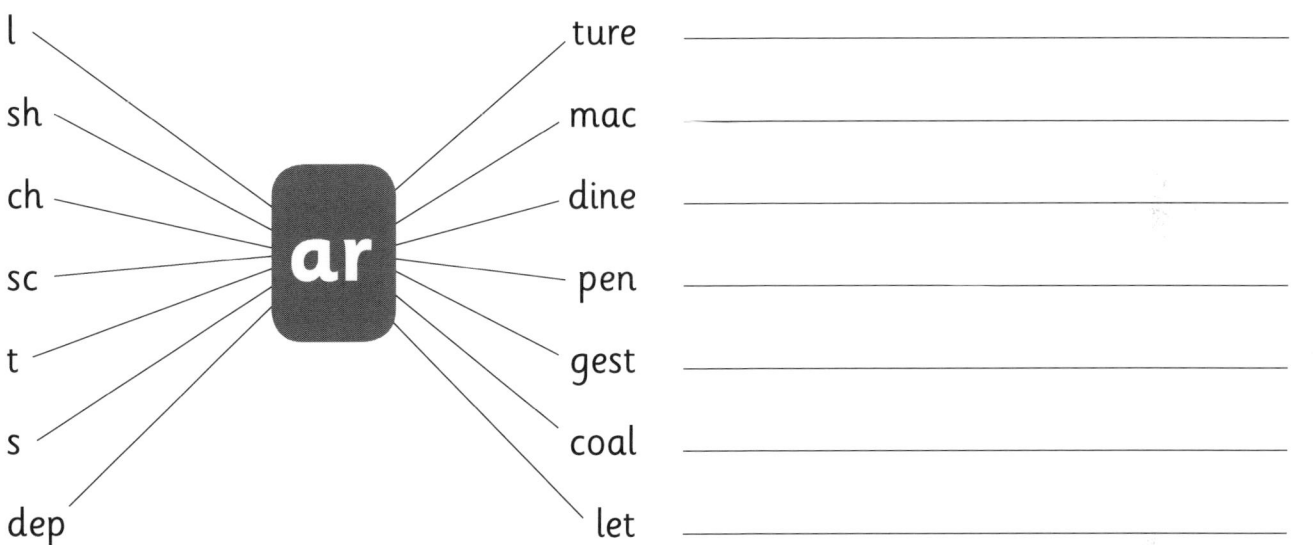

CLUES

1. a tinned fish
2. setting off on a journey
3. used for road surfaces
4. bright red
5. make into a point
6. charred wood
7. biggest

© David Moseley and Gwyn Singleton 2015 | *ACE Spelling Activities* | LDA | Permission to photocopy

Using ACE

Spellings for sounds puzzles

*The sound /**air**/ as in RARE BEAR*

Can you follow the lines below to join the beginnings and endings of the words to the middle sound /**air**/?

Remember that the sound /**air**/ will be spelt in different ways, so check the words in the *ACE Spelling Dictionary* before you write them down.

When you have found all seven words, you can use them to fill in the crossword puzzle.

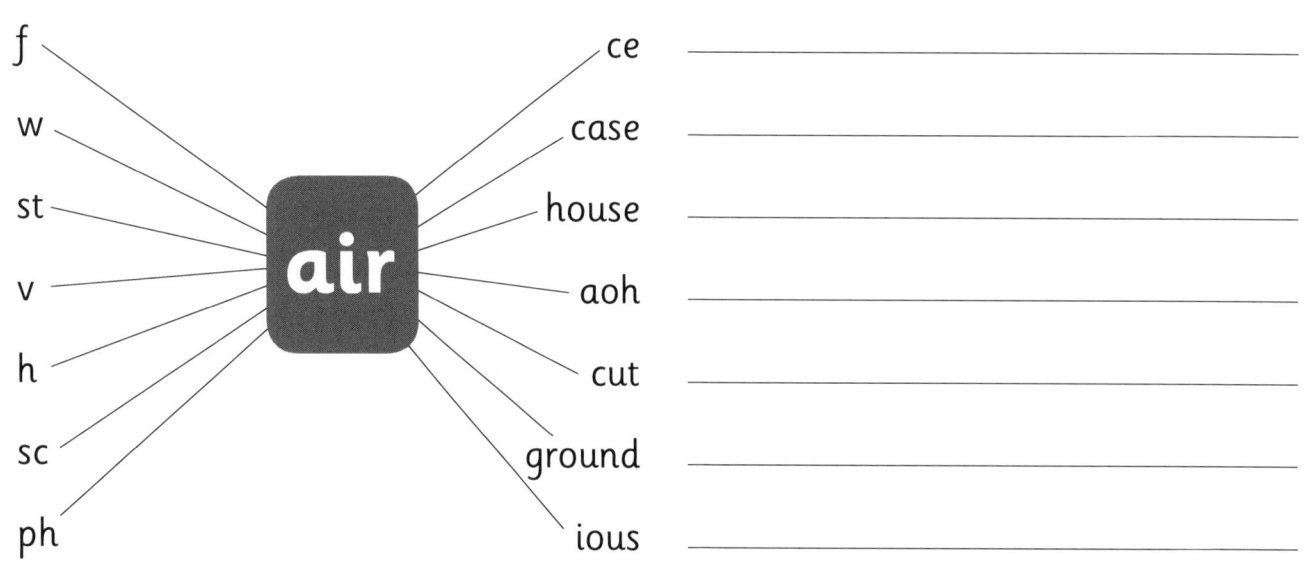

CLUES

1. in short supply
2. building for storing goods
3. ruler of ancient Egypt
4. a barber's handiwork
5. steps from floor to floor
6. of different kinds
7. amusement park

Spellings for sounds puzzles

The sound /er/ as in EARLY BIRD WITH WORM

Can you follow the lines below to join the beginnings and endings of the words to the middle sound /**er**/?

Remember that the sound /**er**/ will be spelt in different ways, so check the words in the *ACE Spelling Dictionary* before you write them down.

When you have found all seven words, you can use them to fill in the crossword puzzle.

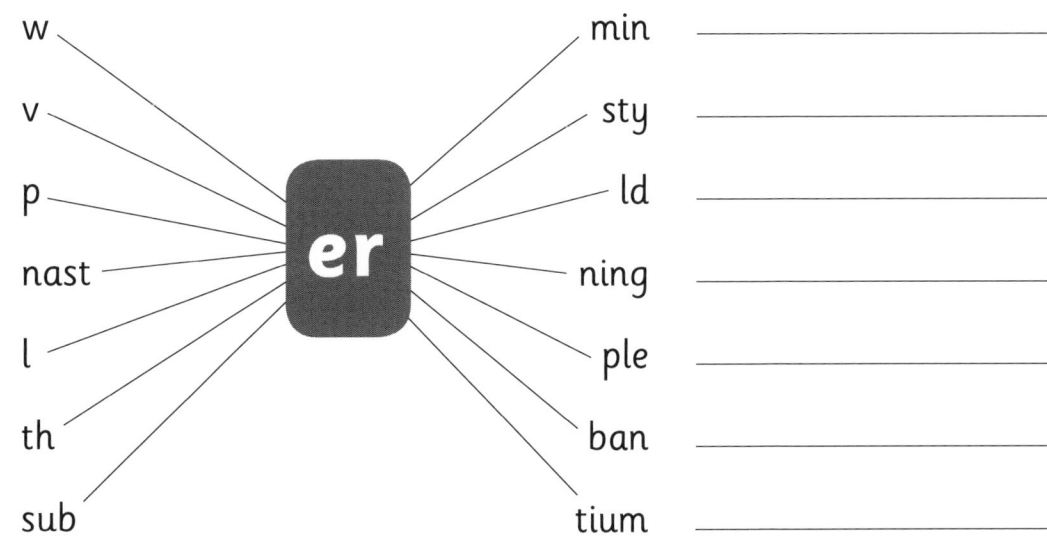

w — min
v — sty
p — ld
nast — ning
l — ple
th — ban
sub — tium

CLUES

1. needing a drink
2. gaining knowledge or skill
3. rats, mice and other pests
4. an orange trumpet-shaped flower
5. of the outer city
6. planet Earth and everything on it
7. a royal colour

Using ACE

Spellings for sounds puzzles

*The sound /**or**/ as in WARLIKE HORSE*

Can you follow the lines below to join the beginnings and endings of the words to the middle sound /**or**/?

Remember that the sound /**or**/ will be spelt in different ways, so check the words in the *ACE Spelling Dictionary* before you write them down.

When you have found all seven words, you can use them to fill in the crossword puzzle.

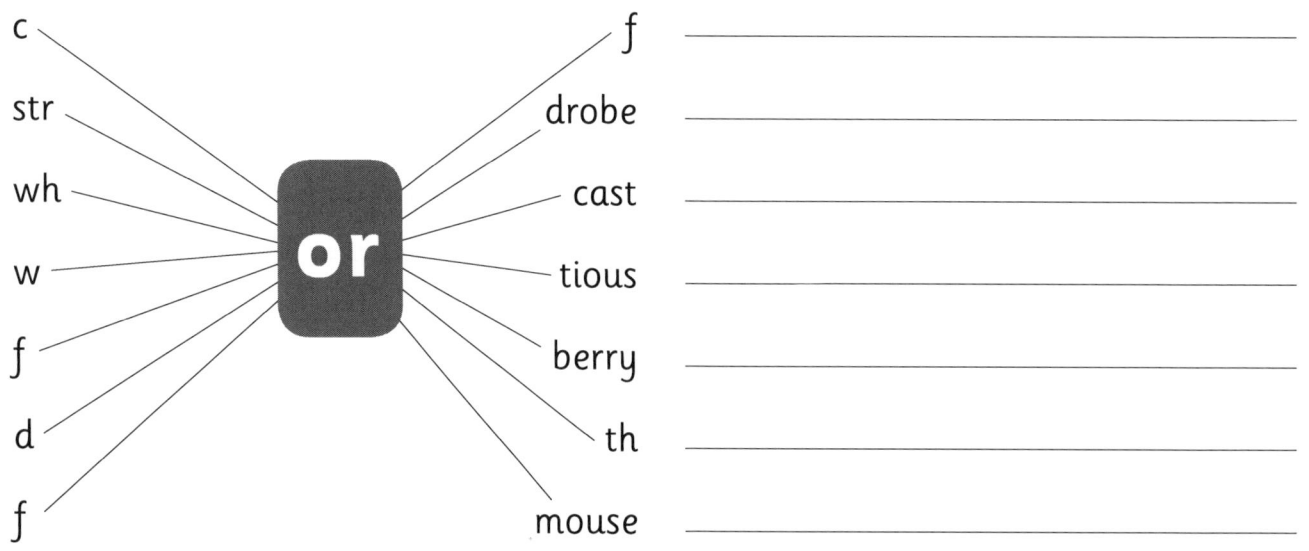

CLUES

1. a small, sleepy country creature

2. nervous and careful

3. a prediction

4. a place where ships unload

5. after third and before fifth

6. a soft red fruit

7. a cupboard for clothes

58

Spellings for sounds puzzles

The sound /oi/ as in JOYFUL OYSTER

Can you follow the lines below to join the beginnings and endings of the words to the middle sound /oi/?

Remember that the sound /oi/ will be spelt in different ways, so check the words in the *ACE Spelling Dictionary* before you write them down.

When you have found all seven words, you can use them to fill in the crossword puzzle.

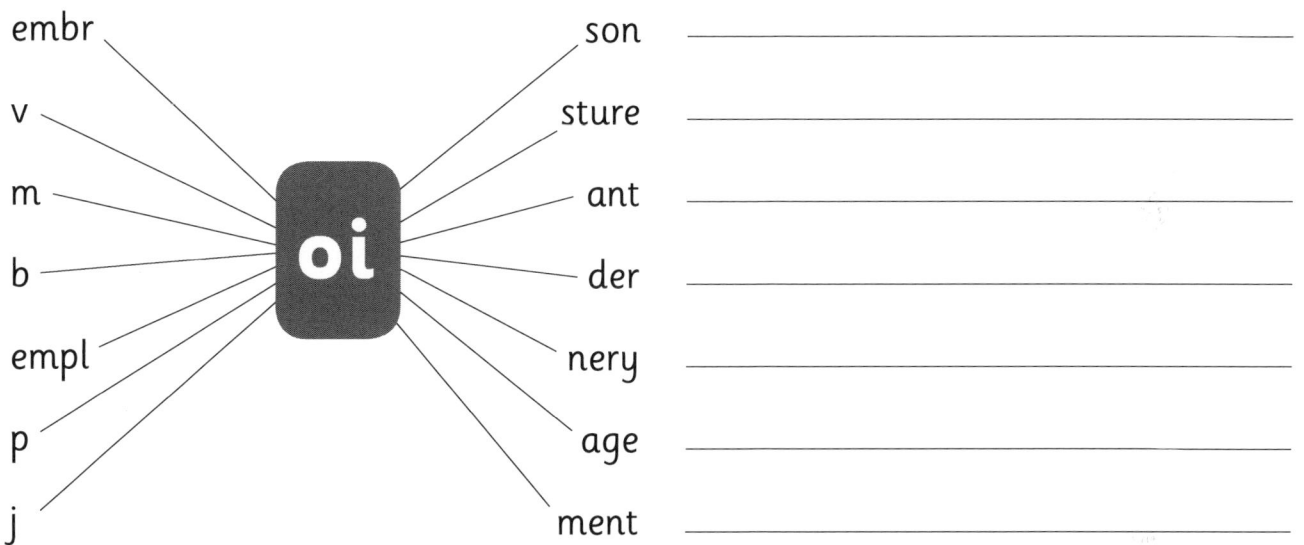

CLUES

1. dampness
2. carpentry on a small scale
3. decorate with stitches
4. able to float easily
5. deadly substance
6. sea journey
7. situation with pay

Using ACE

Spellings for sounds puzzles

The sound /ou/ as in AN OWL SOUND

Can you follow the lines below to join the beginnings and endings of the words to the middle sound /**ou**/?

Remember that the sound /**ou**/ will be spelt in different ways, so check the words in the *ACE Spelling Dictionary* before you write them down.

When you have found all seven words, you can use them to fill in the crossword puzzle.

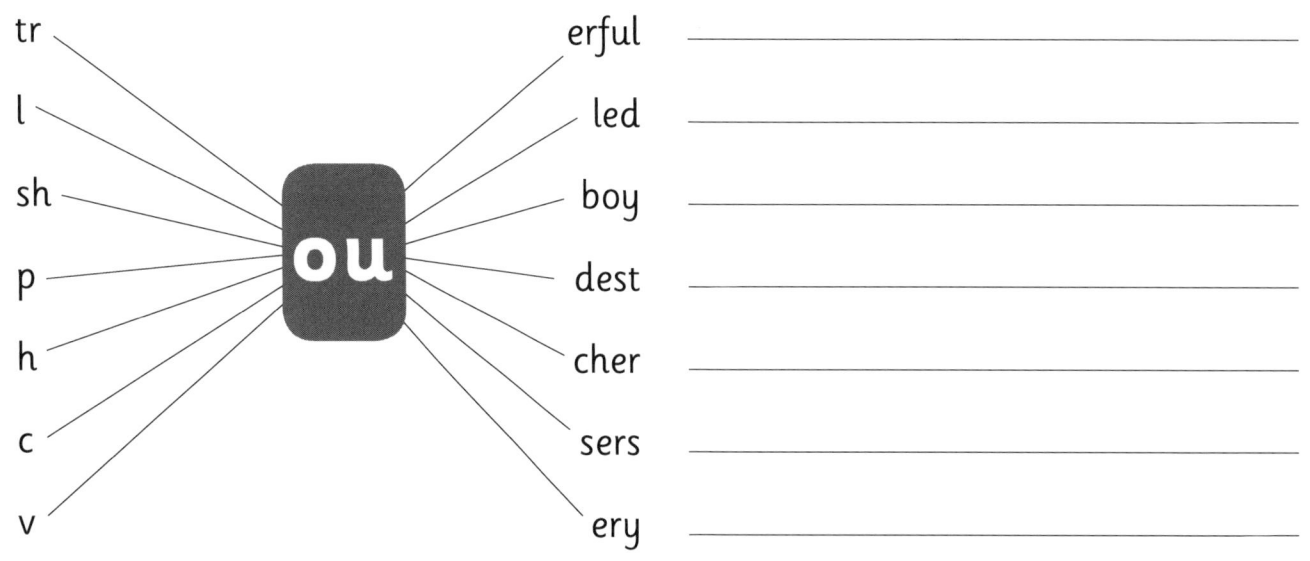

CLUES

1. cried like a wolf
2. noisiest
3. herder of cattle
4. a ticket worth money
5. full of strength
6. garment worn on legs
7. rainy

60

Using ACE

Car registration games 1

Find words which include these car registration letters. The first letter must be the first letter in the word and the last letter the last letter of the word. You are also given an ACE vowel sound which is included in the word, but you are not told how that sound is spelt.

You will be able to find all the answers in the *ACE Spelling Dictionary* if you turn to the right page. All the words have two syllables (**).

CLUES

e.g.	JKY	(dog)	o	page 103	*jockey*
1.	HVY	(elephant)	e	page 40	_ _ _ _ _
2.	BCN	(snail)	ae	page 138	_ _ _ _ _
3.	BDY	(dog)	o	page 95	_ _ _ _
4.	RWD	(horse)	or	page 266	_ _ _ _ _
5.	WMN	(owl)	oo	page 136	_ _ _ _ _
6.	BLT	(snail)	ae	page 138	_ _ _ _ _ _
7.	RPN	(lion)	ie	page 189	_ _ _ _ _
8.	SCT	(eagle)	ee	page 169	_ _ _ _ _

Now complete the square, using the eight words you have made.

CLUES

1. a breakfast food
2. a female person
3. a prize
4. a piece of jewellery worn around the wrist
5. you have one, dead or alive
6. hard to lift
7. something hidden or unrevealed
8. to grow towards perfection, as fruit does

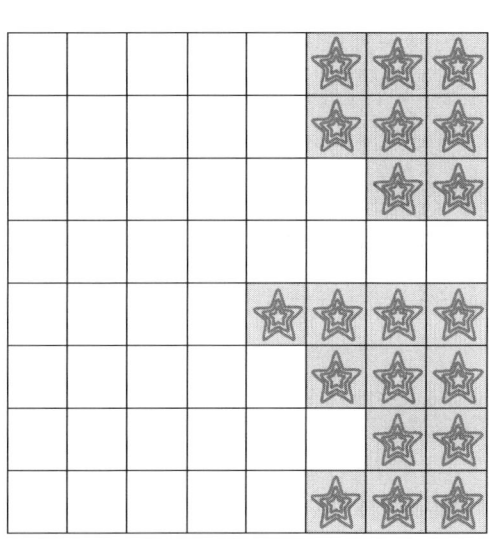

© David Moseley and Gwyn Singleton 2015 | *ACE Spelling Activities* | LDA | Permission to photocopy

Using ACE

Car registration games 2

Find words which include these car registration letters. The first letter must be the first letter in the word and the last letter the last letter of the word. You are also given an ACE vowel sound which is included in the word, but you are not told how that sound is spelt.

You will be able to find all the answers in the *ACE Spelling Dictionary* if you turn to the right page. All the words have two syllables (**).

CLUES

e.g.	CBY	ou	page 227	*cowboy*
1.	KTP	e	page 42	__ __ __ __ __ __ __
2.	NHL	ie	page 187	__ __ __ __ __ __ __
3.	OTH	o	page 107	__ __ __ __ __ __ __
4.	EHT	or	page 259	__ __ __ __ __ __ __
5.	FSN	a	page 12	__ __ __ __ __ __ __
6.	WPL	er	page 255	__ __ __ __ __ __ __
7.	RSN	ee	page 167	__ __ __ __ __ __ __
8.	WKT	i	page 92	__ __ __ __ __ __ __

Now complete the square, using the eight words you have made.

CLUES

1. swirling water
2. fumes from a car
3. a long-legged bird
4. dusk followed by darkness
5. sauce
6. a popular style
7. an explanation for something
8. a target you bowl at in cricket

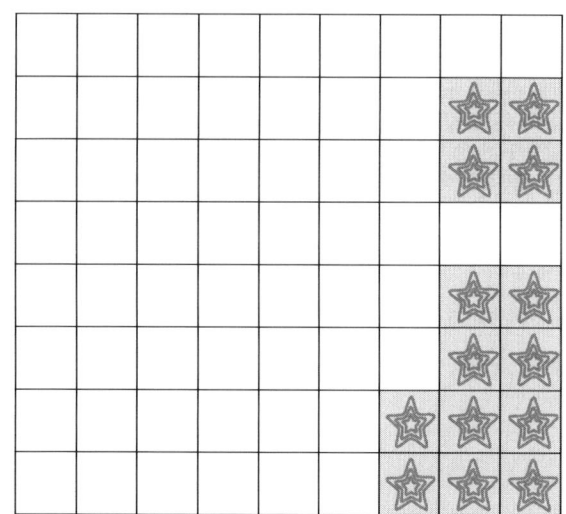

Using ACE

Car registration games 3

Find words which include these car registration letters. The first letter must be the first letter in the word and the last letter the last letter of the word. You are also given an ACE vowel sound which is included in the word, but you are not told how that sound is spelt.

You will be able to find all the answers in the *ACE Spelling Dictionary* if you turn to the right page. All the words have two syllables (**).

CLUES

e.g.	RHG	🦅 ee	page 167	*reaching*
1.	LPD	🐘 e	page 43	_ _ _ _ _ _
2.	DNF	🐱 a	page 10	_ _ _ _ _ _
3.	OCN	🐐 oe	page 203	_ _ _ _ _
4.	GGS	🐴 or	page 261	_ _ _ _ _ _
5.	JFY	🐷 i	page 77	_ _ _ _ _
6.	RBY	🐊 ue	page 220	_ _ _ _
7.	RNR	🐌 ae	page 148	_ _ _ _ _ _
8.	DGN	🦢 u	page 120	_ _ _ _ _ _

Now complete the square, using the eight words you have made.

CLUES

1. an animal with antlers
2. a precious red stone
3. an underground prison
4. lovely
5. a great expanse of water
6. a moment
7. dead skin among hair
8. a wild animal with spots

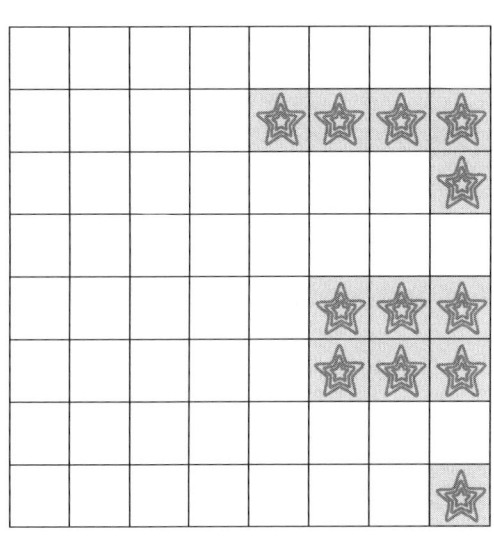

Using ACE

Tricky word endings — 1

The vowel spellings are missing in these words, but each word ends with a neutral vowel sound, spelt 'ar', 'er' or 'or'. You must work out the answers from the clues and check them (especially the endings) in the *ACE Spelling Dictionary* or in the wordsearch below. Write in the missing vowel spellings.

CLUES

1. the person who keeps an eye on prisoners   j _ _ l _ _
2. a machine that sets something in motion   m _ t _ _
3. a tool or handle to start a machine or raise something   l _ v _ _
4. a person who does not tell the truth   l _ _ _
5. someone who gives something (e.g. blood)   d _ n _ _
6. a tall support   p _ ll _ _

Find the above six words in the wordsearch and circle them. Can you find and circle another four words with neutral vowel endings? The words go in the following directions: → ↓ ↘

```
p  e  f  l  a  r  i  q  s  o
d  t  e  f  a  r  m  e  r  t
l  g  p  i  r  s  o  n  a  e
e  d  o  u  v  o  t  e  r  n
s  p  o  d  o  n  o  r  a  j
l  c  i  i  n  u  r  o  z  a
e  a  t  l  b  k  l  e  o  i
v  s  u  n  l  c  a  i  r  l
e  c  k  f  y  a  i  l  a  e
r  l  m  o  w  e  r  s  t  r
```

Now write out six of the words you have found and think of a word which rhymes with each. The rhyming words do not have to end with the same spelling, but the endings must sound the same, e.g. 'peculiar' with 'Julia'. Check the spellings in the *ACE Spelling Dictionary* before you write the words down.

1. _____ rhymes with _____
2. _____ rhymes with _____
3. _____ rhymes with _____
4. _____ rhymes with _____
5. _____ rhymes with _____
6. _____ rhymes with _____

Tricky word endings 2

The vowel spellings are missing in these words, but each word ends with a neutral vowel sound, spelt 'an', 'en', 'in' or 'on'. You must work out the answers from the clues and check them (especially the endings) in the *ACE Spelling Dictionary* or in the wordsearch below. Write in the missing vowel spellings.

CLUES

1. to become firm and solid	h __ d __ __
2. to become stronger	t __ __ gh __
3. a relative	c __ __ s __ __
4. salted pork	b __ c __ __
5. to cover with the darkest colour	bl __ ck __ __
6. claw of a bird of prey	t __ l __ __

Find the above six words in the wordsearch and circle them. Can you find and circle another four words with neutral vowel endings? The words go in the following directions: → ↓ ↘

e	b	l	a	c	k	**e**	**n**	d	o
s	r	i	p	w	r	s	t	o	s
d	y	s	t	o	r	u	n	s	e
c	e	b	i	m	e	t	r	i	a
w	o	e	h	**a**	r	d	**e**	**n**	s
a	b	u	p	**n**	s	i	s	i	**o**
y	a	s	s	e	t	a	l	**o**	**n**
o	c	c	a	**i**	**n**	t	l	e	d
r	**o**	t	t	**e**	**n**	r	e	f	i
s	**n**	u	t	o	u	g	h	**e**	**n**

Now write out six of the words you have found and think of a word which rhymes with each. The rhyming words do not have to end with the same spelling, but the endings must sound the same, e.g. 'dozen' with 'cousin'. Check the spellings in the *ACE Spelling Dictionary* before you write the words down.

1. _____ rhymes with _____
2. _____ rhymes with _____
3. _____ rhymes with _____
4. _____ rhymes with _____
5. _____ rhymes with _____
6. _____ rhymes with _____

Using ACE

Tricky word endings — 3

The vowel spellings are missing in these words, but each word ends with 'cian', 'sion' or 'tion'. You must work out the answers from the clues and check them (especially the endings) in the *ACE Spelling Dictionary* or in the wordsearch below. Write in the missing vowel spellings.

CLUES

1. country	n _ _ _ _ n
2. job	_ cc _ p _ _ _ _ n
3. crash	c _ l _ _ _ _ _ n
4. meeting of court	s _ s _ _ _ n
5. movement	m _ _ _ _ n
6. strong feeling	p _ s _ _ _ _ n
7. person who does clever tricks	m _ g _ _ _ _ _ n
8. a shortened word	_ bbr _ v _ _ _ _ _ n
9. answer to a problem	s _ l _ _ _ _ _ n
10. a person who makes and sells glasses	_ pt _ _ _ _ _ n

Find and circle in the wordsearch the ten words listed above. Can you find and circle another three words with 'tion' endings? The words go in the following directions: → ↓ ↘

m	o	t	i	o	n	l	f	a	v	o	t
a	b	b	r	e	v	i	a	t	i	o	n
g	p	c	r	e	a	t	s	i	o	c	o
i	a	o	p	t	i	f	v	a	p	c	p
c	s	l	t	s	a	u	e	l	t	u	s
i	s	l	b	i	n	t	x	o	i	p	e
a	i	i	w	f	o	r	a	t	c	a	s
n	o	s	u	r	e	n	t	i	i	t	s
i	n	i	l	t	o	d	i	o	a	i	i
o	s	o	l	u	t	i	o	n	n	o	o
n	i	n	a	t	i	o	n	t	o	n	n
s	f	c	r	e	t	h	n	s	i	d	e

© David Moseley and Gwyn Singleton 2015 | *ACE Spelling Activities* | LDA | Permission to photocopy

Using ACE

Tricky word endings 4

The vowel spellings are missing in these words, but each word ends with 'ary', 'ery' or 'ory'. You must work out the answers from the clues and check them (especially the endings) in the *ACE Spelling Dictionary* or in the wordsearch below. Write in the missing vowel spellings.

CLUES

1.	finding something new	d __ sc __ v __ r __
2.	a place where young children are cared for	n __ __ s __ r __
3.	good enough	s __ t __ sf __ ct __ r __
4.	highly unusual	__ xtr __ __ d __ n __ r __
5.	getting something back	r __ c __ v __ r __
6.	expressing praise	c __ mpl __ m __ nt __ r __
7.	great skill	m __ st __ r __
8.	a written account of the past	h __ st __ r __
9.	raining from time to time	sh __ __ __ r __
10.	defeat of an enemy	v __ ct __ r __

Find and circle in the wordsearch the ten words listed above. Can you find and circle another five words with 'ary', 'ery' or 'ory' endings? The words go in the following directions: → ↓

w	d	i	s	c	o	v	**e**	**r**	**y**	e	r	y
e	m	b	r	o	i	d	**e**	**r**	**y**	a	h	e
v	n	a	v	m	e	m	o	r	h	g	s	s
e	u	x	i	p	m	i	l	t	i	r	d	t
r	r	n	c	l	a	e	n	v	s	a	i	m
y	s	a	t	i	s	f	a	c	t	**o**	**r**	**y**
s	**e**	l	**o**	m	t	e	r	y	**o**	r	e	s
h	**r**	o	r	e	**e**	n	t	s	**r**	d	c	t
o	**y**	i	**y**	n	**r**	v	o	r	**y**	i	t	**e**
w	a	n	n	t	**y**	t	a	r	y	n	**o**	**r**
e	x	t	r	**a**	o	r	d	i	n	**a**	**r**	**y**
r	u	r	e	r	e	c	o	v	**e**	**r**	**y**	o
y	e	y	a	**y**	i	n	e	t	r	y	p	t

Using ACE

Doubles or singles 1

Can you complete the words below? You are given the first two sounds, including the vowel.

Try both short and long sounds and see if you can think of an answer that fits the meaning. When you complete the words you will need to decide between single and double consonants: 'l' or 'll', 'm' or 'mm', 'n' or 'nn', 'p' or 'pp', 't' or 'tt'. Use the *ACE Spelling Dictionary* to check your answers, or to search for an answer if you are stuck.

MEANING	BEGINNING	WRITE
1. way, method of behaviour	ma	
2. hot seasoning	pe	
3. person in charge of an aeroplane	pi	
4. a toy you ride by pushing with one foot	scoo	
5. metal object shot from a gun	bu	
6. has been put down on paper	wri	
7. a tool for hitting nails	ha	
8. the front fold of a jacket or blazer	la	
9. a yellow spread for bread	bu	
10. a carved American Indian pole	to	

Do the double consonants follow a particular type of vowel sound?

Are there any exceptions to the rule?

Doubles or singles 2

Can you complete the words below? You are given the first two sounds, including the vowel.

Try both short and long sounds and see if you can think of an answer that fits the meaning. When you complete the words you will need to decide between single and double consonants: 'l' or 'll', 'm' or 'mm', 'n' or 'nn', 'p' or 'pp', 't' or 'tt'. Use the *ACE Spelling Dictionary* to check your answers, or to search for an answer if you are stuck.

	MEANING	BEGINNING	WRITE
1.	a green salad vegetable	le	
2.	a person's rank in a group	sta	
3.	to tease or vex	a	
4.	lavatory	toi	
5.	a large passenger boat	li	
6.	a person who plays the drums	dru	
7.	excellent	su	
8.	a citrus fruit	le	
9.	sickness	il	
10.	a glowing light around a saint's head	ha	

Do the double consonants follow a particular type of vowel sound?

Are there any exceptions to the rule?

Find the middle syllable

The short /a/ sound as in ACTIVE CAT

Sometimes the middle of a long word is the hardest part to spell.

This exercise will help you to spell difficult longer words. Say the words slowly and clearly to yourself and fill in the missing letters.

You can check all your answers by looking in the *** (three-syllable) columns of the *ACE Spelling Dictionary*.

CLUES		WRITE
e.g. a hard-fired paint	e _ _ _ el	*enamel*
1. a device to help you float safely to earth	par _ chute	
2. twisted and caught up	en _ _ _ gled	
3. an unmarried man	bach _ lor	
4. eye makeup	mas _ _ ra	
5. brave, courageous	val _ ant	
6. picture made by sewing on canvas	tap _ _ try	
7. a spear thrown at a sports event	jav _ lin	
8. a large warship	bat _ _ _ ship	
9. taking numbers away	sub _ _ _ tion	
10. to make a product well-known	ad _ _ tise	
11. to desert, to leave	a _ _ _ don	
12. a cloth or tissue for wiping the nose	hand _ _ _ chief	
13. in a furious manner	an _ _ _ ly	
14. living creatures	an _ mals	
15. well-known	fa _ _ iar	

Find the middle syllable

The short /e/ sound as in HEALTHY ELEPHANT

Sometimes the middle of a long word is the hardest part to spell.

This exercise will help you to spell difficult longer words. Say the words slowly and clearly to yourself and fill in the missing letters.

You can check all your answers by looking in the *** (three-syllable) columns of the *ACE Spelling Dictionary*.

CLUES		WRITE
e.g. recall of events and experiences	mem __ ry	*memory*
1. one who examines a thing carefully	ins __ __ tor	
2. skin colour and appearance	com __ __ __ ion	
3. framework of bones	skel __ ton	
4. rubber boot	wel __ __ __ ton	
5. severely frighten	ter __ __ fy	
6. easily hurt or broken	del __ cate	
7. fun and laughter	mer __ __ ment	
8. instructions for preparing food	rec __ pe	
9. a punishment	pen __ __ ty	
10. deer meat	ven __ son	
11. a place to eat	res __ __ rant	
12. able to bend easily	flex __ ble	
13. unpleasant, attack	of __ __ sive	
14. someone who expects the worst	pes __ __ mist	
15. scale of temperature	Cel __ __ us	

Find the middle syllable

The short /i/ sound as in BIG PIGLET

Sometimes the middle of a long word is the hardest part to spell.

This exercise will help you to spell difficult longer words. Say the words slowly and clearly to yourself and fill in the missing letters.

You can check all your answers by looking in the *** (three-syllable) columns of the *ACE Spelling Dictionary*.

CLUES		WRITE
e.g. person who performs tricks	ma __ cian	*magician*
1. high-ranking soldier	brig __ dier	
2. long-legged pink bird	fla __ __ go	
3. delicately beautiful	ex __ __ ite	
4. not taking proper care	ne __ __ __ ful	
5. dangerous or evil-looking	sin __ __ ter	
6. weakly joined and easily broken	rick __ y	
7. small river flowing into a larger one	trib __ tary	
8. an ice-cream flavour	va __ __ la	
9. purpose or plan	in __ __ tion	
10. handgun	re __ __ ver	
11. go on happening	con __ __ ue	
12. a choice or judgment	de __ __ sion	
13. opposite of multiplication	di __ sion	
14. talking something over with someone	dis __ __ sion	
15. very hard	dif __ cult	

Find the middle syllable

The short /o/ sound as in WATCHFUL DOG

Sometimes the middle of a long word is the hardest part to spell.

This exercise will help you to spell difficult longer words. Say the words slowly and clearly to yourself and fill in the missing letters.

You can check all your answers by looking in the *** (three-syllable) columns of the *ACE Spelling Dictionary*.

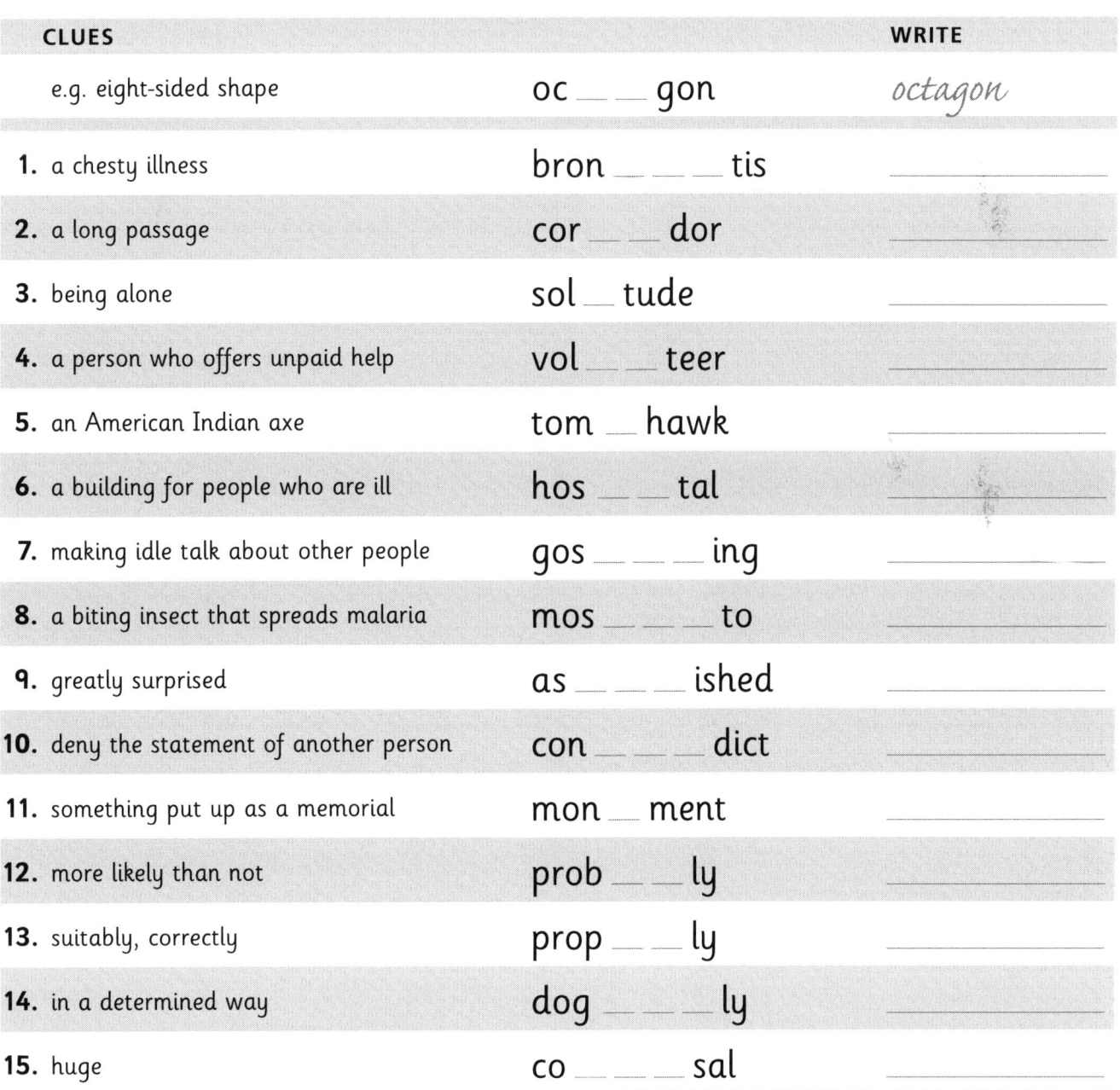

CLUES		WRITE
e.g. eight-sided shape	oc __ __ gon	*octagon*
1. a chesty illness	bron __ __ __ tis	
2. a long passage	cor __ __ dor	
3. being alone	sol __ tude	
4. a person who offers unpaid help	vol __ teer	
5. an American Indian axe	tom __ hawk	
6. a building for people who are ill	hos __ __ tal	
7. making idle talk about other people	gos __ __ __ ing	
8. a biting insect that spreads malaria	mos __ __ __ to	
9. greatly surprised	as __ __ ished	
10. deny the statement of another person	con __ __ __ dict	
11. something put up as a memorial	mon __ ment	
12. more likely than not	prob __ __ ly	
13. suitably, correctly	prop __ __ ly	
14. in a determined way	dog __ __ __ ly	
15. huge	co __ __ sal	

Using ACE

Find the middle syllable

The short /u/ or /oo/ sound as in DUCK AND WOODPECKER

Sometimes the middle of a long word is the hardest part to spell.

This exercise will help you to spell difficult longer words. Say the words slowly and clearly to yourself and fill in the missing letters.

You can check all your answers by looking in the *** (three-syllable) columns of the *ACE Spelling Dictionary*.

CLUES		WRITE
e.g. unwilling to do something	re ___ ctant	*reluctant*
1. a large cow-like animal	buf ___ lo	
2. a soccer player	foot ___ er	
3. the art of preparing hot food	cook ___ y	
4. marvellous	won ___ ful	
5. a large honey-making insect	bum ___ bee	
6. person who buys something	cus ___ er	
7. news report	bull ___ in	
8. increase in number	mul ___ ply	
9. lacking awareness through the senses	un ___ scious	
10. guessing about what is happening	won ___ ing	
11. one-storey house	bun ___ low	
12. one more of the same kind	an ___ er	
13. try to stop by showing disapproval	dis ___ age	
14. a dried seedless grape	sul ___ na	
15. quickly and unexpectedly	sud ___ ly	

Find the middle syllable

The long /ae/ sound as in BABY SNAIL

Sometimes the middle of a long word is the hardest part to spell.

This exercise will help you to spell difficult longer words. Say the words slowly and clearly to yourself and fill in the missing letters.

You can check all your answers by looking in the *** (three-syllable) columns of the *ACE Spelling Dictionary*.

CLUES		WRITE
e.g. small peach-like fruit	a _ _ _ cot	*apricot*
1. calmly and without complaining	pa _ _ _ _ ly	
2. stone parts of a building	ma _ _ _ ry	
3. envelopes and writing material	sta _ _ _ ery	
4. great surprise or wonder	a _ _ _ ment	
5. storyteller	nar _ _ tor	
6. fixing a name to	la _ _ ling	
7. in error	mis _ _ ken	
8. local area	neigh _ _ _ hood	
9. likely to cause harm	dan _ _ _ ous	
10. large serving spoon	ta _ _ spoon	
11. in a trembling manner	sha _ _ ly	
12. unable to wait	im _ _ tient	
13. a holiday period	va _ _ tion	
14. annoyed disappointment	frus _ _ tion	
15. large sports area for spectators	sta _ _ um	

Find the middle syllable

The long /ee/ sound as in BREEDING EAGLE

Sometimes the middle of a long word is the hardest part to spell.

This exercise will help you to spell difficult longer words. Say the words slowly and clearly to yourself and fill in the missing letters.

You can check all your answers by looking in the *** (three-syllable) columns of the *ACE Spelling Dictionary*.

CLUES		WRITE
e.g. programme written in parts	se _ _ al	*serial*
1. came before	pre _ _ ded	
2. successful outcome	a _ _ _ _ _ _ ment	
3. strong and passionate	ve _ ment	
4. tiredness	wea _ ness	
5. a means of land transport	ve _ _ cle	
6. boring and tiring	te _ _ ous	
7. coming earlier in time or order	pre _ _ ous	
8. food in the form of grain	ce _ _ al	
9. restore confidence	re _ sure	
10. even-handedly, to the same degree	eq _ _ _ ly	
11. too proud, puffed up	con _ _ _ _ ed	
12. landscape features	scen _ ry	
13. gentle, merciful	le _ _ ent	
14. with genuine feeling	sin _ _ _ _ ly	
15. newspapers, television and radio	me _ _ a	

Find the middle syllable

The long /ie/ sound as in LIVELY LION

Sometimes the middle of a long word is the hardest part to spell.

This exercise will help you to spell difficult longer words. Say the words slowly and clearly to yourself and fill in the missing letters.

You can check all your answers by looking in the *** (three-syllable) columns of the *ACE Spelling Dictionary*.

CLUES		WRITE
e.g. a very hard precious stone	di __ mond	*diamond*
1. causing lively feelings	ex __ __ ing	
2. moving home each season	mi __ __ ting	
3. a three-sided shape	tri __ __ gle	
4. a musical instrument with flat bars	xy __ phone	
5. a collection of books	li __ __ ry	
6. task	as __ __ __ ment	
7. amazingly huge	gi __ __ tic	
8. the line where sky and earth meet	ho __ __ zon	
9. way of earning a living	live __ hood	
10. joyfully successful	tri __ phant	
11. the material of elephant tusks	i __ ry	
12. offering something to influence judgment	bri __ ry	
13. to do with money	fi __ __ cial	
14. a person who prepares a plan	de __ __ __ er	
15. someone who remains alive after danger	sur __ vor	

Using ACE

Find the middle syllable

The short /oe/ sound as in LONELY GOAT

Sometimes the middle of a long word is the hardest part to spell.

This exercise will help you to spell difficult longer words. Say the words slowly and clearly to yourself and fill in the missing letters.

You can check all your answers by looking in the *** (three-syllable) columns of the *ACE Spelling Dictionary*.

CLUES		WRITE
e.g. left out	o _____ ted	*omitted*
1. a strong (usually pleasant) smell	a _____ ma	
2. unable to move	im _____ bile	
3. lawful possession	ow _____ ship	
4. steady affection, strong commitment	de _____ tion	
5. food and household supplies	gro _____ ries	
6. leaves	fo _____ age	
7. very bad, shocking	a _____ cious	
8. friendly, liking company	so _____ ble	
9. lacking and wanting human contact	lone _____ ness	
10. a strong feeling	e _____ tion	
11. hateful, repulsive, very unpleasant	o _____ ous	
12. a large, fibre-covered nut	co _____ nut	
13. fierce	fe _____ cious	
14. cheerily good-natured, jolly	jo _____ al	
15. an orchestral stringed instrument	vi _____ la	

Find the middle syllable

The /oo/ and /ue/ sounds as in SMOOTH NEWT

Sometimes the middle of a long word is the hardest part to spell.

This exercise will help you to spell difficult longer words. Say the words slowly and clearly to yourself and fill in the missing letters.

You can check all your answers by looking in the *** (three-syllable) columns of the *ACE Spelling Dictionary*.

	CLUES		WRITE
	e.g. eager to find out, unusual	cu __ ous	*curious*
1.	where old things may be displayed	mu __ __ um	
2.	a rude, noisy troublemaker	hoo __ __ gan	
3.	an exact copy	du __ __ cate	
4.	shaped like a hollow pipe	tu __ __ lar	
5.	a pleasant pastime	a __ __ __ ment	
6.	a time of celebration to mark an event	ju __ __ lee	
7.	a person who goes by car or train to work	com __ __ ter	
8.	apply oil	lu __ __ __ cate	
9.	causing destruction, decayed	ru __ __ ous	
10.	containing or worked by air	pneu __ __ __ ic	
11.	lovely	beau __ __ ful	
12.	someone who enters without permission	in __ __ der	
13.	very quiet and private	se __ __ ded	
14.	a person escaping from capture	fu __ __ tive	
15.	shining in the dark	lu __ __ nous	

Using ACE

Find the middle syllable

using all sections of the Dictionary

Sometimes the middle of a long word is the hardest part to spell.

This exercise will help you to spell difficult longer words. Say the words slowly and clearly to yourself and fill in the missing letters.

You can check all your answers by looking in the *** (three-syllable) columns of the *ACE Spelling Dictionary*.

CLUES		ANIMAL PICTURE CLUE	WRITE
e.g. a food not unlike butter	mar ___ rine		*margarine*
1. a pair of glasses	spec ___ cles		
2. tired out, completely used up	ex ___ ed		
3. full of energy	vig ___ ous		
4. a person who designs buildings	ar ___ tect		
5. a clear, fizzy drink	lem ___ ade		
6. a two-wheeled machine	bi ___ cle		
7. wonderful	mar ___ lous		
8. a large ape	go ___ la		
9. breaking in and stealing	bur ___ ry		
10. a person from another country	fo ___ er		
11. musicians under a conductor	or ___ tra		
12. a picture made with small tiles	mo ___ ic		
13. definitely	cer ___ ly		
14. full of very high hills	moun ___ ous		
15. an arrangement to meet	ap ___ ment		

Find the two middle syllables

using all sections of the Dictionary 1

Sometimes the middle of a long word is the hardest part to spell.

This exercise will help you to spell difficult longer words. Say the words slowly and clearly to yourself and fill in the missing letters.

You can check all your answers by looking in the **** (four-syllable) columns of the *ACE Spelling Dictionary*.

CLUES		ANIMAL PICTURE CLUE	WRITE
e.g. not natural, man-made	ar _ _ _ _ cial		*artificial*
1. triumphant in battle	vic _ _ _ _ ous		
2. not achievable	im _ _ _ _ _ ble		
3. the total of inhabitants	pop _ _ _ tion		
4. surroundings	en _ _ _ _ _ ment		
5. process of growing or changing	de _ _ _ _ _ ment		
6. a belief based on ignorant fear	su _ _ _ _ _ _ tion		
7. capturing images on camera	pho _ _ _ _ _ phy		
8. exactly the same	i _ _ _ _ cal		
9. absurd	ri _ _ _ lous		
10. looking or sounding good	fa _ _ _ _ ble		
11. a measurement of distance	kil _ _ _ tre		
12. the smallest part of a group	mi _ _ _ _ ty		
13. making a person feel awkward	em _ _ _ _ _ _ ing		
14. public commemoration	me _ _ _ al		
15. unplanned, done on impulse	spon _ _ _ _ ous		

Using ACE

Find the two middle syllables

using all sections of the Dictionary ❷

Sometimes the middle of a long word is the hardest part to spell.

This exercise will help you to spell difficult longer words. Say the words slowly and clearly to yourself and fill in the missing letters.

You can check all your answers by looking in the **** (four-syllable) columns of the *ACE Spelling Dictionary*.

CLUES		ANIMAL PICTURE CLUE	WRITE
e.g. clever	in _____ gent		*intelligent*
1. well-known for something bad	no _____ ous		_____
2. a ceremony of crowning	co _____ tion		_____
3. to build up or collect	ac _____ late		_____
4. not lasting	tem _____ ry		_____
5. owner of a business or building	pro _____ tor		_____
6. savings in outgoing costs	e _____ mies		_____
7. make known	com _____ cate		_____
8. plant growth	veg _____ tion		_____
9. causing much laughter	hi _____ ous		_____
10. study of the heavenly bodies	as _____ my		_____
11. large self-service store	su _____ ket		_____
12. meat-eating	car _____ rous		_____
13. a severe throat infection	ton _____ tis		_____
14. strange, special	pe _____ ar		_____
15. at right angles to vertical	hor _____ tal		_____

Words within words 1

Find the baseword or simplest form of each word and write it in the box. To do this remove the word ending.

Then, using the *ACE Spelling Dictionary*, find another word which starts with the baseword and write it on the line. The longer word must have at least three more letters than the baseword.

Take care with double consonants and with basewords which end with a 'magic e'.

CLUES	BASEWORD	WRITE
e.g. sunny	*sun*	*sunburnt*
1. safety		
2. careless		
3. fitted		
4. funniest		
5. rocky		
6. thundered		
7. netting		
8. raindrop		
9. downwards		
10. earthed		
11. shopper		
12. slipped		
13. footstep		
14. brightly		
15. sometimes		

Using ACE

Words within words 2

Find the baseword or simplest form of each word and write it in the box. To do this remove the word ending.

Then, using the *ACE Spelling Dictionary*, find another word which starts with the baseword and write it on the line. The longer word must have at least three more letters than the baseword.

Take care with double consonants and with basewords which end with a 'magic e'.

CLUES	BASEWORD	WRITE
e.g. thirsty	*thirst*	*thirstiness*
1. centimetre		
2. dirty		
3. cheerfully		
4. signing		
5. wholemeal		
6. dreaded		
7. infectious		
8. personal		
9. favourite		
10. governor		
11. schooling		
12. greedy		
13. timer		
14. pointer		
15. agreeable		

Find the baseword or root   1

Basewords are simple words from which others derive their meaning. You can often find them on the same page of the *ACE Spelling Dictionary* as the words based on them.

Underline the correct meaning of each numbered word. Write the root or baseword in the box.

CLUES

e.g. the baseword for **personality** is **person**

e.g. the baseword for **leadership** is **lead**

#	Word	Meanings	Baseword
1.	politely	a) in a well-mannered way b) in a clever way	
2.	explosion	a) unprotected from the weather b) a loud noise when something is blown up	
3.	miner	a) less important b) a mineworker	
4.	plantation	a) a large group of trees grown by people b) a garden centre	
5.	cheater	a) a person who breaks rules for profit b) a fast-running animal	
6.	scornfully	a) walking painfully on sore feet b) mockingly	
7.	globally	a) circular in shape b) worldwide	
8.	reliable	a) able to relay a message b) dependable	
9.	simplicity	a) an uncomplicated state b) stupidity	
10.	fictitious	a) fierce b) invented, untrue	

Using ACE

Find the baseword or root — 2

Basewords are simple words from which others derive their meaning. You can often find them on the same page of the *ACE Spelling Dictionary* as the words based on them.

Underline the correct meaning of each numbered word. Write the root or baseword in the box.

CLUES

e.g. the baseword for **numerous** is **number**

e.g. the baseword for **migration** is **migrate**

1. mortally	a) made with bricks and mortar b) fatally	
2. liberation	a) the experience of being set free b) a group of librarians	
3. joyfully	a) showing pleasure and excitement b) joining two things	
4. optician	a) someone who looks on the bright side b) someone who tests eyesight	
5. navigator	a) an explorer b) someone who chooses the correct direction	
6. review	a) a survey or critical account b) a second chance	
7. streamer	a) a little stream b) a paper decoration	
8. employee	a) someone who offers work b) someone who gets paid for work	
9. lessen	a) reduce b) a period of instruction	
10. accepted	a) not included b) received	

Using ACE

Introducing the parts of speech

NOUNS 1

Words which can have 'a' or 'the' in front of them are used to name things. They are nouns. In this exercise all the words which fill the gaps are nouns. The *ACE Spelling Dictionary* page number is given to help you find them, together with the number of syllables.

PAGE 138

★★	**1.** The fire _____ was called out after the explosion.
★	**2.** At last the fierce _____ was extinguished.
★	**3.** Each pony has a _____ of hay in its stable.
★★	**4.** He gave his wife a silver necklace and _____.

PAGE 200

★★	**1.** The air _____ demonstrated the safety drill.
★★	**2.** We stayed in a _____ near the beach.
★	**3.** Grandma did not want to live in a retirement _____.
★★	**4.** We use a _____ to wash the car.

PAGE 120

★	**1.** My little brother likes to bang his toy _____.
★★	**2.** The baby cries if she loses her _____.
★★★	**3.** It doesn't matter if I get dirt on my _____.
★	**4.** The white _____ cooed on the window-sill.

PAGE 246

★★★	**1.** Dad bought new _____ for my bedroom.
★	**2.** I gave Mum a pretty green _____ in a pot.
★★	**3.** Metals are heated in a _____.
★★★★	**4.** Horse manure is an organic _____.

© David Moseley and Gwyn Singleton 2015 | *ACE Spelling Activities* | LDA | Permission to photocopy

Using ACE

Introducing the parts of speech

NOUNS 2

Words which can have 'a' or 'the' in front of them are used to name things. They are nouns. In this exercise all the words which fill the gaps are nouns. The *ACE Spelling Dictionary* page number is given to help you find them, together with the number of syllables.

PAGE 164

* **1.** Mum brought some _____ for Sunday lunch.

** **2.** The weighing _____ did not speak the truth.

** **3.** The doctor said my spots were the _____.

* **4.** We went to a restaurant for a _____.

PAGE 240

* **1.** The bus went round the _____.

** **2.** I stuffed an old suit to make a _____.

* **3.** My brother made me do my _____ of the washing-up.

** **4.** We carried the bed up the _____.

PAGE 212

*** **1.** The boy carried the _____ into the church.

*** **2.** I bought some new games for my _____.

*** **3.** We had ham and _____ sandwiches.

* **4.** The detective looked for a _____ to the murder.

PAGE 277

* **1.** There was not a _____ in the sky.

*** **2.** The town _____ made a long speech.

* **3.** The Queen wears a _____ when she opens Parliament.

* **4.** I lay on the _____ to watch my favourite TV programme.

Introducing the parts of speech

VERBS 1

A verb often follows a noun (or a pronoun such as 'we') to express an action (actual or possible), thought or feeling. In this exercise all the words which fill the gaps are verbs. The *ACE Spelling Dictionary* page number is given to help you find them, together with the number of syllables.

PAGE 142

**	1.	We _____ the cake with chocolate.
*	2.	I think that photograph should be enlarged and _____.
**	3.	I knew the TV was broken when the picture _____ away.
**	4.	Dad _____ us for borrowing his camera without permission.

PAGE 46

*	1.	The hen began to _____ at the food.
**	2.	He _____ his parents for a new phone.
***	3.	She was on her bike, _____ very fast.
*	4.	We _____ on, trying to make up lost time.

PAGE 277

**	1.	I was _____ my sweets when the baby grabbed one.
**	2.	The injured man _____ as the soldier raised his rifle.
*	3.	It is time to _____ the carnival queen.
**	4.	We _____ into the lift instead of using the stairs.

PAGE 133

**	1.	It was hard going, _____ up the steep hill.
*	2.	My dog _____ its tail when I opened a tin of its favourite food.
***	3.	The moles in the garden are always _____ away.
*	4.	Don't _____ that cake until teatime.

Using ACE

Introducing the parts of speech

VERBS ②

A verb often follows a noun (or a pronoun such as 'we') to express an action (actual or possible), thought or feeling. In this exercise all the words which fill the gaps are verbs. The *ACE Spelling Dictionary* page number is given to help you find them, together with the number of syllables.

PAGE 252

** **1.** I was _____ all over town for some new trainers.

* **2.** I _____ the pancake mixture thoroughly.

** **3.** The _____ sea heaved the small boat against the rocks.

* **4.** He had to _____ to avoid hitting the traffic island.

PAGE 192

* **1.** I could _____ simple knots when I was five.

*** **2.** The teacher _____ French lessons for Friday mornings.

* **3.** She _____ to phone her mum, but the phone was out of signal.

* **4.** I shall _____ the race with my stopwatch.

PAGE 154

** **1.** The invading army _____ the town.

* **2.** She will buy a stud farm and _____ racehorses.

* **3.** We could hardly _____ in the crowded room.

* **4.** We hoped that we would _____ the record.

PAGE 96

** **1.** We spent all morning _____ wood.

* **2.** Make sure there's no traffic before you _____ the road.

** **3.** He did not _____ on her appearance.

*** **4.** Please don't _____ my plans by trying to change them.

Introducing the parts of speech

ADJECTIVES

Adjectives are words which add to the meaning of names like persons, places, ideas or things. They often answer a question such as 'What is it like?'. In this exercise all the words which fill the gaps are adjectives. The *ACE Spelling Dictionary* page number is given to help you find them, together with the number of syllables.

PAGE 188

** **1.** She rudely turned down my _____ request.

** **2.** I would love my own _____ helicopter.

** **3.** Do hypnotists really have _____ powers?

*** **4.** Five-year-olds go to _____ school.

PAGE 24

*** **1.** That big lion looks _____.

*** **2.** The _____ shed was blown down in a gale.

** **3.** My clothes were torn and _____.

** **4.** _____ numbers are called out in a bingo session.

PAGE 113

** **1.** Some chemical waste is highly _____.

*** **2.** The _____ rainforests are being destroyed.

** **3.** Ben won a _____ apple at the fair.

** **4.** I have got a _____ headache.

PAGE 263

** **1.** Brian was put on the _____ step as a punishment.

** **2.** A body temperature of 37° Celsius is completely _____.

*** **3.** Sailors used to rely on _____ charts.

** **4.** The Tyne is a river in _____ England.

Using ACE

Introducing the parts of speech

ADVERBS

Adverbs are words which add to the meaning of verbs or adjectives. Many of them end in 'ly'. They answer questions such as 'How?', 'How much?', 'Where?' and 'When?'. In this exercise all the words which fill the gaps are adverbs. The *ACE Spelling Dictionary* page number is given to help you find them, together with the number of syllables.

PAGE 134

*****   1. _____, my teacher was worried about my nosebleed.

******   2. Julie was always dressed _____.

****   3. Bouncer was _____ the best dog in the show.

***   4. The ground was rough and stony _____.

PAGE 190

**   1. Sharon came forward _____ to receive her prize.

******   2. The experimental results must be analysed _____.

***   3. The small boy nodded _____.

****   4. _____, they won all three matches.

PAGE 52

*****   1. The traffic lights were _____ out of action.

****   2. The violin solo was _____ very difficult.

****   3. It rained _____ for three hours.

***   4. After the party we were _____ late to bed.

PAGE 28

***   1. I replied very _____, so as not to give offence.

***   2. They died _____ in a car crash.

*****   3. The dictator ruled _____ for 25 years.

***   4. She _____ accepted the seat he gave up for her.

Searching for patterns

Here are some further ideas for your students, to help them recognise some of the many spelling patterns and the exceptions!

1. When you add **ing** to words ending with **e**, you knock off the **e**. This does not apply if the ending is **ee** or **oe**. See how many words you can find in two minutes that fit this pattern.

2. See how many three-syllable words you can find where a final **y** changes to an **ie**. Group these under the headings: **ies**, **ied** and **ier/iest**.

3. With words like **wit** (with a one-letter vowel and a single final consonant) you double the final consonant when you add endings such as **ed**, **ing**, **er**, **est**, **y**, **ier** and **iest**. So you get: slow-**witted**, out**witting**, **witty**, **wittier**, **wittiest**.

   See how many one-syllable words you can find in ten minutes that fit this pattern. Are there any exceptions?

4. Find ten words like **itch** (one syllable, with a single letter short vowel and the /**tch**/ sound right after the vowel).

   Find ten more one-syllable words with a letter between the short vowel and the /**ch**/ sound, such as **belch**, **inch**, **lunch**.

   Find 20 words ending in **ch** from any of the long vowel sections.

   What pattern do you notice? Are there any exceptions, apart from **rich**, **much** and **such**? Can you explain in a simple way when to use **tch**?

   Carry out similar searches in order to establish when to use **dge** rather than **ge** and when to use **ck** rather than **k**.

5. Think about this spelling rule: **i** before **e** except after **c**. What is the ratio of hits to misses if this rule is applied to words in the long vowel /**ee**/ section?

6. How many words of four or more syllables in which the last syllable contains a neutral vowel sound can you find in five minutes?

7. Make a list of homonym pairs from the /**or**/ section where spelling confusion is likely.

8. truthful – truthfully
   helpful – helpfully
   grateful – gratefully

   Full of ...? Find five more words listed in the *ACE Spelling Dictionary* that fit this pattern.

Learning spellings

Words you need to know

Some of the words you meet every day are not easy to write. 'Friend' is one of those unfriendly words. Words which break the law should be treated with suspicion. You need to use an IDENTIKIT card to check the special features of these suspect words. The master list of suspects is on page 95.

What to do

1. Put a tick next to each word on the list which you know very well. These words are innocent and may even be friendly. The others will make up your list of suspects. You will find that some of the suspects have split personalities and may seem to be two separate words, although they are really only one.

2. Get a piece of card which will fit into your *ACE Spelling Dictionary* or into your notebook if folded down the middle.

3. Copy your list of suspects, with further particulars if provided, in two columns. You can add some words of your own if you want to. Then use a highlighter pen to mark any special features of the suspect words which will help you to remember them.

4. Make a second copy of your list of suspects on the back of your card, but this time do not add the further particulars. Leave a space or draw a box beside each word so that you can tally marks to show how many times you have recognised a suspect.

5. Ask a friendly word-inspector to check your IDENTIKIT card when it is ready for use.

6. Get to know your suspects better. Take four words at a time and make up some sentences using these words. Write out your sentences and when you get to a suspect word, find it on your card so you can copy it. Try to copy it after looking at it only once and as you write it notice any special features. When you have finished, ask your friendly word-inspector to double-check what you have written, using your card and the *ACE Spelling Dictionary* if necessary.

How to use your IDENTIKIT card

Get out your card every time you do some writing. Whenever a suspect word comes along, check it on your card before you write it down. Every time you do this, turn your card over and put a tally mark next to the word. You can cross off suspect words when you no longer need to check them on your card, but you should not do this until you have at least ten tally marks against a word.

IDENTIKIT master list of suspect words

again		right	(✓ or →)
always	(all _ _ _)	running	
an	(a .. e .. i .. o .. u ..)	sometimes	
another		still	
bought		stopped	
caught	(did catch)	suddenly	
decided		their	(ownership)
friend		there	(there is …
heard	(_ ear _)		there are …
hour	(60 minutes)		there was …
inside			there were …
into			there will be …
it's	(it is)		there would be …
kept			there could be … etc.
knew	(silent k)	⟶	to or in that place)
know	(silent k)	thought	
lot	(a lot)	through	(by way of)
might	(?igh?)	too	(too much/as well)
myself		tried	
off	(not on)	turned	
opened		until	(_ _ till)
outside		want	
police		were	(in the past)
		where	(place)

It is a good idea to make a new IDENTIKIT card once a term until you have narrowed down your list of suspects to one or two dangerous individuals. If you succeed in doing this you will have reduced the crime rate by up to 20%.

Learning spellings

How to remember the special features of the most dangerous suspects

always	This is **always** one word with one **l**, all the time.
an	An egg, **an** anything beginning with **a e i o u**.
caught	Her naughty daughter **caught** a cold.
heard	Did hear, by **ear**.
hour	60 minutes.
it's	**It's** short for 'it is' and the ' stands for the letter **i**.
knew	(silent **k**) – understood.
know	(silent **k**) – understand?
lot	'**A lot**' is NOT one word.
might	I **might** get it right!
off	On and off, '**off**' is confused with '**of**'.
right	Did you write it on the **right** and get it **right**?
their	Our dog is ours, not yours – **their** dog is theirs.
there	Here and **there there** are some rare bears.
through	Although it was rough, he thought we would get **through**.
too	Not TOO many **o**'s to count in twos!
until	One **l** as in **1-nil**: unlike fill, hill, kill, pill, till, will.
were	Why **were** we waiting when the light was green?
where	**Where** were you when the fire broke out in that place?

Learn to spell these really useful words

and get them right when you write!

Three lists of 220 useful words each have been prepared from samples of children's speech and writing. The lists do not include the 40 most commonly misspelt high-frequency words. These can be found on page 95 and are best learned by using the IDENTIKIT card in the course of writing. Simple words which present no spelling problems have been left out. Taken together, the three lists plus the 40 IDENTIKIT words account for between 40% and 60% of the words found in children's writing at ages 9–11.

Each list can be covered in one term, at the rate of 20 words a week. This allows for some repeated learning of words misspelt in weekly tests. Students who need an accelerated spelling programme can work on the lists for a whole year.

It is recommended that useful hard-to-spell words as well as chosen interesting words should be entered into the *ACE Spelling Word Bank*. There is room for up to 1500 words to be added into the Word Bank.

Using the three lists

It is not intended that the same list should be given to all members of a class. All three lists are needed in order to provide for a typical range of ability and teachers may want to add others which are more or less demanding. The following tests can be used to decide which list should be used by which students.

Learning spellings

Spelling test

Say each word, repeat it in a phrase or sentence, pause briefly and then say the word again.

1.	SHIP	... The passengers boarded the SHIP	...	SHIP
2.	FOOTBALL	... My FOOTBALL strip	...	FOOTBALL
3.	READING	... What are you READING?	...	READING
4.	TELL	... TELL me a story	...	TELL
5.	SEVEN	... SEVEN puppies in a basket	...	SEVEN
6.	SPOKE	... I SPOKE to Gran on the phone	...	SPOKE
7.	SLOWLY	... We walked very SLOWLY	...	SLOWLY
8.	NEAR	... We live NEAR the park	...	NEAR
9.	PERSON	... Who is that PERSON crossing the road?	...	PERSON
10.	ANYTHING	... Have you ANYTHING to report?	...	ANYTHING
11.	PRETTY	... The garden was looking very PRETTY	...	PRETTY
12.	BEFORE	... Tidy your room BEFORE you go out	...	BEFORE
13.	OWNER	... Who is the OWNER of this car?	...	OWNER
14.	MUSIC	... I listen to MUSIC on my phone	...	MUSIC
15.	HAPPENED	... What HAPPENED in the playground?	...	HAPPENED
16.	FOLLOWED	... The stray dog FOLLOWED me	...	FOLLOWED
17.	SUGAR	... SUGAR in your tea	...	SUGAR
18.	MOUNTAIN	... The top of the MOUNTAIN	...	MOUNTAIN
19.	USUAL	... I woke up at seven, as USUAL	...	USUAL
20.	INTERESTING	... An INTERESTING story	...	INTERESTING

Students scoring:

0–4 should work with List 1

5–14 should work with List 2

15–20 should work with List 3

The 220 words in each list have been grouped into sets of four words, on the basis of a topic or language pattern. There are five word sets across the page; five sets are enough for a week's work. Nouns, verbs, adjectives and adverbs have been grouped together, with some miscellaneous sets at the end. This makes it easier to think of meaningful links between words and to use the words in sentences.

Note that words with an asterisk (*) against them may need special attention, as it is hard or impossible to find a rhyming word with the same spelling pattern. You may be able to think of a non-rhyming word with the same letter string (e.g. watch/match) or find some other way of remembering the letters.

The word sets are not arranged in order of difficulty.

Individual lists

Students can follow individual paths, so that they do not study words they can already spell. The alphabetical lists can be used in this way, preferably in conjunction with the *ACE Spelling Word Bank*.

Every fortnight, students choose 20, 40 or 60 words to learn from one of the lists. These are words which the student would like to be able to spell. The words are underlined and then written down in sets of four. If possible, there should be some meaningful link between the words in a set, as this makes the words and their spellings easier to remember. Students can choose words that will fit into a sentence, that are linked by topic or that have the same spelling pattern. Searching in the *ACE Spelling Dictionary* or the *ACE Spelling Word Bank* will make it easy to put together groups of four words with the same spelling pattern.

Regular testing of small groups of words learned in a daily routine is essential. This can be organised in pairs, with students testing each other. It is not advisable to give the same spelling test to a whole class.

After a test, selected words can be entered into a personal *ACE Spelling Word Bank*. These words may serve either as a celebration of successful learning or as prompts for further study.

Spelling patterns for vowels are the main source of difficulty in English spelling. Grouping words by their vowel sound or vowel spelling is an excellent way of making learning more effective.

Another kind of individual list, for use in correcting drafts, is described on pages 101–102.

How to learn

If you look at words in a list and have someone test you, you may not remember the spellings very well. A more active approach will lead to better results. You should **STUDY**, **COPY**, **CHECK**, **HIGHLIGHT** and then **LEARN**. Try the different methods of learning given below and decide which work best for you.

STUDY	look at the word and count the syllables
COPY	you are allowed only one glance per syllable
CHECK	letter by letter or in strings of up to four letters
HIGHLIGHT	mark the parts you need to remember
LEARN	by one or more of these methods:

a) pronounce the words in a different way, according to the spelling
b) trace over or write the word, saying the letter names before you write each letter string
c) shut your eyes and say or spell the word as you 'write' it in large letters with your finger
d) with eyes shut see the word in your mind, count the letters in groups and then check
e) study the word so well that you can spell it backwards

Learning spellings

f) study the word, say a tongue-twister or count to ten, then spell the word
g) think of a memory link or mnemonic for the whole word or just for the tricky part (e.g. On **Fri**day and at the week**end** I'll see my friends. **F**ind **R**eally **I**nteresting **FRI**ends.)
h) look for a common word ending, such as an **es** plural and **ed** tense ending, or **y** changing to **ies** or **ied**
i) use the *ACE Spelling Dictionary* to find a word which rhymes with the one you are learning and is spelt in the same way. Think of a rhyme and then check the spelling, or simply look through the one- and two-syllable columns in a single vowel section (**Note**: words marked * do not have suitable rhymes)
j) find another word you already know which has the same spelling pattern, (e.g. tongue, argue)
k) learn the tricky part (or parts) first, before trying the whole word.

REPEAT   say, write and spell really rapidly, like a R-A-PP-E-R
TEST   look, cover, write, check

At the end of a learning session, write down a sentence containing the words you have studied. This may help you to spell those words correctly later on when you are writing – which is the whole point!

The daily routine

Every day you will study two, four or six words from your list. It is helpful if the words are related in some way. Enter the date and the words to be learned in a notebook.

Steps to success

1st word	learn (using chosen method)
self-test	look, cover, write, check
2nd word	learn
self-test	look, cover, write, check
double-check	look at both words, cover, write, check
	Continue if both words are correct; otherwise, practise and try the test again
3rd word	learn
self-test	look, cover, write, check
4th word	learn
self-test	look, cover, write, check
double-check	look at both words, cover, write, check
	Continue if both words are correct; otherwise, practise and try the test again
final test	all four words should be written correctly when dictated in a random order

If you do not pass the final test, you must try to learn the words again, perhaps by a different method. On the other hand, it may be better to attempt two words instead of four.

When you succeed on the final test, a responsible person should initial the list in your notebook and record the learning method(s) from a) to k).

If you find four words easy to learn, you might like to work with groups of six instead.

Note that if you are trying to learn six words you can double-check with groups of two or three words.

The weekly test

Once a week, test sessions should be set up in pairs, so that each learner both gives and receives a test on the 8, 16 or 24 words chosen for that week. Words spelt correctly should be given a tick in the notebook and on the master list. Those not spelt correctly may be studied again the following week, but if so they should be spaced out over the week.

Spelling correctly and correcting mistakes

If you use the **STUDY**, **COPY**, **CHECK**, **HIGHLIGHT**, **LEARN** approach, you will probably make fewer mistakes with words you have recently studied. You can hardly expect that you will never have to think about those words again. Indeed, every time you realise that you have used a word that is on your list or seems to fit a familiar pattern, you score a success. All you then have to do is to check the spelling. If it is correct, that is EXCELLENT!

Good spellers are aware of common patterns between 'families' of words. The more often you look up words in the *ACE Spelling Dictionary* or enter new words in the *ACE Spelling Word Bank*, the more you will notice these patterns. Looking for word families based on Lists 1–3 can introduce you to thousands of words. Learning method i) (looking up rhyming words) is one of the best ways of getting to know more word families. This method also encourages you to use a wider vocabulary when you write.

Most people miss spelling mistakes when they read through a piece of work. You can improve at this if you make a personal alphabetical list of the words you want to learn from Lists 1, 2 and 3. It is sensible to include some interesting words from the same 'families' and any hard-to-spell words you have previously attempted. If you arrange the list in syllable columns, as in the *ACE Spelling Dictionary*, it will be easier to scan. Read through the list before you check your draft: this will make it much more likely that you will recognise the words in the piece you have written.

Learning spellings

Your list might look like this:

*	**	*** (+)
aren't	against	ambulance
board	allow	arrival
break	answer	beautiful
brought	answered	disappeared
clothes	believe	February
course	buried	hospital
guard	curtain	idea
it's	harbour	investigate
knocked	haunted	parliament
let's	later	remembered
passed	people	suitable
past	present	unfortunately
piece	quickly	vegetables
race	really	
spare	swimming	
they're	themselves	
threw	without	
you're		

It is a good idea to check your draft at least three times, each time concentrating on a limited range of words. First, look for any words of three or more syllables which need to be checked. Then go through the passage again, looking for two-syllable words which might present problems. Finally, concentrate on one-syllable words, taking care not to skim over words such as **it's**, **they** and **was** which do not 'leap off the page'.

The more often you correct your own spelling mistakes, the better your spelling will become. When you know how to put things right, you can really concentrate on what you are writing.

List 1

Number of words: 220

father	* baby	dog	bus	money
dad	babies	hair	car	gold
mother	boy	way	road	bank
mum	girl	park	street	shop
look	ask	come	be	* are
looked	asked	* coming	been	will
find	call	came	* being	could
found	called	went	stay	couldn't
one	some	bad	* front	* his
* two	left	good	ready	* her
three	all	better	nice	our
four	more	best	happy	your
garden	door	tea	book	king
farm	room	water	story	queen
wood	window	time	bed	lady
sea	fire	things	night	man
go	* was	woke	see	catch
goes	* wasn't	help	saw	make
* going	would	told	* put	made
gone	wouldn't	sleep	seen	eat
black	big	next	my	away
blue	little	last	* this	around
red	new	long	that	back
white	old	round	other	home
* children	* morning	* Christmas	* woman	* people
sister	* afternoon	tree	teacher	name
brother	week	day	school	hand
* aunt	year	dinner	work	* eyes
do	* has	give	dance	* watch
don't	* have	gave	walk	* watching
did	* having	take	walking	start
* didn't	had	took	walked	started
when	how	first	no	by
just	so	* once	yes	for
now	down	out	* very	with
then	here	over	well	without
giant	he	him	* who	please
* castle	she	himself	* someone	me
ghost	we	you	which	* that's
house	they	them	* something	much
play	named	like	upon	or
playing	think	married	about	but
played	say	live	* from	* because
fell	* said	* lived	after	while

Learning spellings

List 2

Number of words: 220

* aeroplane	animals	present	* clothes	prince
air	bird	balloon	* body	princess
plane	snake	* colour	* shoes	life
* world	* horse	* music	foot	love
tell	listen	read	point	hold
spoke	listened	reading	write	* build
shouted	* answer	mean	writing	built
hear	* answered	meant	written	* covered
* these	high	* every	wide	* usual
those	* higher	its	* straight	* different
any	smaller	sure	near	* interesting
many	short	true	real	* coloured
wife	* family	* sugar	boat	* football
* husband	table	* breakfast	ship	field
* person	chair	meat	shape	line
* group	* kitchen	* course	* owner	* corner
hope	pick	drop	try	* finish
hoped	picked	dropped	trying	* finished
hoping	pull	break	cry	leave
getting	* pulled	* breaking	cried	fly
* young	whole	tired	dead	* nearby
* beautiful	closed	* lonely	broken	* maybe
* pretty	past	dark	dry	quite
dear	seven	* careful	strange	alright
* machine	dragon	ears	* word	* radio
wheel	head	nose	* idea	station
hole	* heart	mouth	* notice	* minutes
light	blood	* voice	* language	* sentence
seemed	die	sitting	meet	should
* imagine	died	waiting	brought	* does
guess	jumped	* happen	passed	* doesn't
* understand	killed	* happened	followed	done
quickly	already	* even	nearly	onto
slowly	behind	* also	* usually	across
early	ever	* really	* finally	along
later	o'clock	enough	together	against
mountain	piece	* numbers	few	* no-one
side	* picture	* nothing	half	* everyone
ice	place	* thousands	* anyone	* everything
winter	* village	* difference	* anything	whose
buy	before	* I'd	* you'd	* what
wear	why	* I'll	* you'll	* what's
used	whether	* I'm	* you're	* let's
grown	* whenever	* I've	* you've	* themselves

List 3

Number of words: 220

mouse	* squirrel	creatures	fish	* chocolate
mice	goat	* butterfly	* rabbit	coffee
* puppy	* wolf	* dinosaur	* potato	flour
* puppies	* elephant	* monster	* potatoes	* apron
wash	* allow	swim	* arrived	threw
washing	* allowed	swimming	* offered	throw
washed	wished	rain	received	blew
dressed	* cannot	raining	grabbed	blow
* basket	lawn	shirt	* drawer	crash
* bowl	flowers	skirt	shelf	surprise
* board	patch	sheet	shelves	fright
brush	* vegetables	* curtain	stairs	* skeleton
fishing	believe	approach	lie	drag
float	* wondering	* recognised	lying	dragged
floated	* realised	remember	lay	* bury
drowned	* investigate	* remembered	laid	* buried
shock	* uncle	* February	* harbour	pony
* ambulance	* cousin	* months	beach	* ponies
* hospital	* grandfather	* holiday	* island	saddle
* oxygen	* neighbours	* Saturday	cave	stable
* climb	push	hopped	* whisper	* burst
tied	* pushed	hopping	* whispered	guard
falling	knocked	pretended	* whistle	* chase
slipped	smashed	hurt	screamed	* disappeared
pencil	* alphabet	* camera	* parliament	noise
* rubber	* calendar	* film	* palace	* policeman
* ruler	fractions	* submarine	television	* uniform
* scissors	* graph	* magazine	* programme	* court
* dangerous	frightening	* favourite	* curious	lazy
* terrible	* poisonous	* orange	spare	dirty
massive	frightened	* purple	* quiet	* impossible
* enormous	scared	* visible	haunted	funny
* telephone	* visitor	* system	switch	flame
* message	* Germany	defence	* contact	volcano
rhyme	* London	* exhibition	* explosion	thunder
* tongue	* countries	* manager	bridge	* lightning
* motor	* excellent	* British	dining	* downstairs
racing	* wonderful	* Chinese	* hungry	* upstairs
tight	* fantastic	* Japanese	fried	* somewhere
* physical	* exciting	* Egyptian	* frozen	* everywhere
* bicycle	* hello	he'd	* aren't	* anyway
bike	* everybody	he'll	we'd	* somehow
race	* quietly	* he's	we'll	* anybody
track	* sixth	* they're	* we're	* somebody

Learning spellings

Alphabetical list 1

Number of words: 220

about	eyes	man	started
after	farm	married	stay
afternoon	father	me	story
all	fell	money	street
are	find	more	take
around	fire	morning	tea
ask	first	mother	teacher
asked	for	much	that
aunt	found	mum	that's
away	four	my	them
babies	from	name	then
baby	front	named	they
back	garden	new	things
bad	gave	next	think
bank	ghost	nice	this
be	giant	night	three
because	girl	no	time
bed	give	now	told
been	go	old	took
being	goes	once	tree
best	going	one	two
better	gold	or	upon
big	gone	other	very
black	good	our	walk
blue	had	out	walked
book	hair	over	walking
boy	hand	park	was
brother	happy	people	wasn't
bus	has	play	watch
but	have	played	watching
by	having	playing	water
call	he	please	way
called	help	put	we
came	her	queen	week
car	here	ready	well
castle	him	red	went
catch	himself	road	when
children	his	room	which
Christmas	home	round	while
come	house	said	white
coming	how	saw	who
could	just	say	will
couldn't	king	school	window
dad	lady	sea	with
dance	last	see	without
day	left	seen	woke
did	like	she	woman
didn't	little	shop	wood
dinner	live	sister	work
do	lived	sleep	would
dog	long	so	wouldn't
don't	look	some	year
door	looked	someone	yes
down	made	something	you
eat	make	start	your

Alphabetical list 2

Number of words: 220

across	early	line	shoes
aeroplane	ears	listen	shirt
against	enough	listened	should
air	even	lonely	shouted
along	ever	love	side
already	every	machine	sitting
alright	everyone	many	slowly
also	everything	maybe	smaller
animals	family	mean	snake
answer	few	meant	spoke
answered	field	meat	station
any	finally	meet	straight
anyone	finish	minutes	strange
anything	finished	mountain	sugar
balloon	fly	mouth	sure
beautiful	followed	music	table
before	foot	near	tell
behind	football	nearby	themselves
bird	getting	nearly	these
blood	group	no-one	those
boat	grown	nose	thousands
body	guess	nothing	tired
break	half	notice	together
breakfast	happen	numbers	true
breaking	happened	o'clock	try
broken	head	onto	trying
brought	hear	owner	understand
build	heart	passed	used
built	high	past	usual
buy	higher	person	usually
careful	hold	pick	village
chair	hole	picked	voice
closed	hope	picture	waiting
clothes	hoped	piece	wear
colour	hoping	place	what
coloured	horse	plane	what's
corner	husband	point	wheel
course	I'd	present	whenever
covered	I'll	pretty	whether
cried	I'm	prince	whole
cry	I've	princess	whose
dark	ice	pull	why
dead	idea	pulled	wide
dear	imagine	quickly	wife
die	interesting	quite	winter
died	its	radio	word
difference	jumped	read	world
different	killed	reading	write
does	kitchen	real	writing
doesn't	language	really	written
done	later	seemed	you'd
dragon	leave	sentence	you'll
drop	let's	seven	you're
dropped	life	shape	you've
dry	light	ship	young

Learning spellings

Alphabetical list 3

Number of words: 220

allow	Egyptian	lie	screamed
allowed	elephant	lightning	sheet
alphabet	enormous	London	shelf
ambulance	everybody	lying	shelves
anybody	everywhere	magazine	shirt
anyway	excellent	manager	shock
approach	exciting	massive	sixth
apron	exhibition	message	skeleton
aren't	explosion	mice	skirt
arrived	falling	monster	slipped
basket	fantastic	months	smashed
beach	favourite	motor	somebody
believe	February	mouse	somehow
bicycle	film	neighbours	somewhere
bike	fish	noise	spare
blew	fishing	offered	squirrel
blow	flame	orange	stables
board	float	oxygen	stairs
bowl	floated	palace	submarine
bridge	flour	parliament	surprise
British	flowers	patch	swim
brush	fractions	pencil	swimming
buried	fried	physical	switch
burst	fright	poisonous	system
bury	frightened	policeman	telephone
butterfly	frightening	ponies	television
calendar	frozen	pony	terrible
camera	funny	potato	they're
cannot	Germany	potatoes	threw
cave	goat	pretended	throw
chase	grabbed	programme	thunder
Chinese	grandfather	puppies	tied
chocolate	graph	puppy	tight
climb	guard	purple	tongue
coffee	harbour	push	track
contact	haunted	pushed	uncle
countries	he'd	quiet	uniform
court	he'll	quietly	upstairs
cousin	he's	rabbit	vegetables
crash	hello	race	visible
creatures	holiday	racing	visitor
curious	hopped	rain	volcano
curtain	hopping	raining	wash
dangerous	hospital	realised	washed
defence	hungry	received	washing
dining	hurt	recognised	we'd
dinosaur	impossible	remember	we'll
dirty	investigate	remembered	we're
disappeared	island	rhyme	whisper
downstairs	Japanese	rubber	whispered
drag	knocked	ruler	whistle
dragged	laid	saddle	wished
drawer	lawn	Saturday	wolf
dressed	lay	scared	wonderful
drowned	lazy	scissors	wondering

Slippery Characters

Both short and long words often have tricky spellings, such as 'often'. Here are 240 words which are often misspelt, in groups of ten. You can find the missing letters by looking up the words in the *ACE Spelling Dictionary*. You have been given the ACE page number, number of syllables and word length to help you. Words 1–20 have only five letters.

	PAGE NUMBER	SYLLABLES	
1.	66	**	_ qu _ _ _
2.	93	**	w _ m _ n
3.	106	**	o _ _ _ n
4.	126	**	m _ n _ _
5.	141	*	_ _ _ _ t
6.	148	*	r _ _ _ n
7.	155	*	ch _ _ f
8.	174	*	w _ i _ d
9.	182	*	g _ _ d _
10.	185	**	l _ _ _ g
11.	189	*	r _ _ me
12.	214	*	g _ _ _ p
13.	240	**	s _ _ _ y
14.	245	**	_ _ _ ly
15.	245	*	_ _ _ th
16.	247	*	h _ _ rd
17.	248	*	l _ _ _ n
18.	249	**	o _ _ _ r
19.	256	**	_ fu _
20.	260	**	f _ _ ty

It's a good idea to copy words you want to learn into your personal spelling bank and use them for learning four at a time and/or checking as described on pages 99–102.

Learning spellings

	PAGE NUMBER	SYLLABLES	
21.	1	**	ac _ _ l
22.	16	**	_ _ ra _ _
23.	29	**	vac _ _ m
24.	32	*	b _ _ _ th
25.	33	**	_ _ nt _ _
26.	37	***	_ n _ _ g _
27.	37	**	e _ _ ept
28.	43	*	_ _ _ th
29.	82	**	pig _ _ n
30.	85	**	r _ _ thm
31.	89	**	sy _ _ _ l
32.	89	**	s _ _ _ _ m
33.	106	***	o _ _ up _
34.	125	***	l _ _ _ _ y
35.	126	**	m _ s _ l _
36.	141	*	_ _ _ th
37.	157	**	ex _ _ _ _
38.	159	***	_ _ n _ _ s
39.	167	**	r _ c _ _ t
40.	176	**	_ _ _ _ v _

It's a good idea to copy words you want to learn into your personal spelling bank and use them for learning four at a time and/or checking as described on pages 99–102.

Learning spellings

	PAGE NUMBER	SYLLABLES	
41.	178	**	d _ _ _ _ _ _ _
42.	183	**	i _ l _ _ d
43.	208	*	_ _ ou _ _
44.	214	**	f _ _ ure
45.	219	**	p _ _ s _ _
46.	223	***	u _ _ b _ _
47.	225	**	_ ns _ _ _
48.	225	**	ar _ ti _
49.	244	**	c _ _ cl _
50.	260	*	f _ _ _ th

	PAGE NUMBER	SYLLABLES	
51.	1	**	ab _ _ n _ _
52.	2	***	am _ t _ _ _
53.	3	**	a _ _ _ _ ct
54.	3	**	av _ r _ _ _
55.	15	*	gram _ _ _
56.	17	***	_ ma _ _ _ _
57.	21	***	n _ _ _ _ _ l
58.	23	**	p _ _ aps
59.	28	***	tra _ _ _ y
60.	31	**	_ _ _ _ _ ss

It's a good idea to copy words you want to learn into your personal spelling bank and use them for learning four at a time and/or checking as described on pages 99–102.

Learning spellings

	PAGE NUMBER	SYLLABLES	
61.	33	***	cen _ _ _ _
62.	35	***	d _ v _ _ _
63.	44	**	men _ _ _ _
64.	46	**	p _ _ _ _ ss
65.	48	***	reg _ l _ _
66.	50	**	_ _ v _ _ _ l
67.	51	**	spe _ _ _ l
68.	51	**	s _ _ _ est
69.	52	*	twe _ _ _ _
70.	54	**	we _ th _

	PAGE NUMBER	SYLLABLES	
71.	88	***	sim _ l _ _
72.	91	**	vi _ _ _ _ s
73.	100	**	f _ _ _ _ _ n
74.	108	***	pop _ _ _
75.	108	**	prom _ _ _
76.	150	*	_ _ a _ _
77.	153	**	_ ch _ _ _
78.	156	**	_ _ _ _ ve
79.	156	**	d _ _ ea _ _
80.	157	**	ex _ _ _ m _

It's a good idea to copy words you want to learn into your personal spelling bank and use them for learning four at a time and/or checking as described on pages 99–102.

Learning spellings

	PAGE NUMBER	SYLLABLES	
81.	167	**	r _ _ e _ _ t
82.	170	**	s _ n _ _ _
83.	172	*	th _ _ v _ _
84.	182	**	h _ gi _ n _
85.	185	**	li _ _ nc _
86.	193	****	_ _ r _ _ _ y
87.	207	**	s _ _ _ ose
88.	222	*	th _ _ _ _ _
89.	225	***	_ _ ti _ l _
90.	226	**	b _ _ g _ _ n

	PAGE NUMBER	SYLLABLES	
91.	226	**	b _ z _ _ _ _
92.	239	**	_ _ _ _ _ h
93.	243	**	b _ _ gl _ _
94.	244	**	c _ _ _ _ n
95.	246	**	f _ _ th _ _
96.	250	**	p _ _ _ _ s _
97.	256	**	_ _ _ w _ _ d
98.	261	**	f _ _ w _ _ d
99.	266	**	q _ _ _ _ er
100.	268	*	th _ _ _ _ _

It's a good idea to copy words you want to learn into your personal spelling bank and use them for learning four at a time and/or checking as described on pages 99–102.

Learning spellings

PAGE NUMBER	SYLLABLES		
101.	1	***	a _ _ _ d _ _ _ _
102.	1	****	ac _ u _ _ _ y
103.	3	***	_ _ _ ar _ nt
104.	3	**	a _ _ _ ch _ _
105.	7	****	cat _ g _ _ _ _
106.	20	**	ma _ _ _ _ ge
107.	25	**	san _ wi _ _ _
108.	33	***	cem _ t _ r _
109.	34	***	def _ n _ t _
110.	38	***	e _ e _ _ ise

PAGE NUMBER	SYLLABLES		
111.	39	***	Fe _ _ _ _ ry
112.	44	***	med _ _ _ n _
113.	46	**	pl _ _ _ _ nt
114.	47	**	p _ _ ss _ r _
115.	47	**	q _ _ _ _ _ n
116.	48	***	rel _ v _ nt
117.	50	**	sent _ n _ _
118.	50	**	sep _ r _ _ _
119.	51	*	str _ _ _ th
120.	56	***	ad _ i _ _ _ n

It's a good idea to copy words you want to learn into your personal spelling bank and use them for learning four at a time and/or checking as described on pages 99–102.

Learning spellings

	PAGE NUMBER	SYLLABLES		
121.	58	**	b __ s __ n __ __ __
122.	59	***	c __ ns __ __ __ __
123.	66	**	__ qui __ __ __ __
124.	71	***	h __ __ __ if __ __
125.	72	**	in __ __ __ __ s __
126.	73	**	int __ __ __ st
127.	80	**	mis __ __ __ __ f
128.	80	**	mi __ spe __ __
129.	81	***	__ mi __ __ __ __ n
130.	82	***	__ __ __ ical

	PAGE NUMBER	SYLLABLES		
131.	82	***	p __ si __ __ __ n
132.	95	***	bro __ __ __ l __
133.	107	***	o __ __ __ s __ t __
134.	108	***	po __ __ __ bl __
135.	133	**	th __ r __ __ __ __
136.	143	**	gr __ t __ f __ __
137.	147	***	o __ __ a __ __ __ __
138.	150	*	__ __ ai __ __ t
139.	155	***	c __ mpl __ t __ __ __
140.	164	****	m __ t __ __ __ __ l

It's a good idea to copy words you want to learn into your personal spelling bank and use them for learning four at a time and/or checking as described on pages 99–102.

Learning spellings

PAGE NUMBER	SYLLABLES		
141.	179	**	de _ _ _ b _
142.	182	**	g _ _ d _ n _
143.	191	**	su _ pr _ _
144.	207	**	sh _ _ ld _
145.	256	**	_ _ th _ _ _ _
146.	215	***	h _ m _ r _ _ s
147.	226	***	b _ _ b _ c _ _
148.	234	**	s _ r _ _ _ nt
149.	235	***	t _ m _ t _ _
150.	261	**	f _ _ w _ _ _

PAGE NUMBER	SYLLABLES		
151.	11	***	emba _ _ _ _ _
152.	14	***	g _ ar _ nt _ _
153.	25	***	_ _ c _ _ f _ _ _
154.	34	**	desp _ r _ _ _
155.	38	***	e _ c _ _ _ _ nt
156.	45	***	ne _ _ _ _ r _
157.	46	***	pr _ j _ _ _ _ _
158.	48	***	_ _ cog _ _ _
159.	48	***	rec _ _ _ end
160.	53	***	_ _ _ _ t _ b _ _

It's a good idea to copy words you want to learn into your personal spelling bank and use them for learning four at a time and/or checking as described on pages 99–102.

Learning spellings

	PAGE NUMBER	SYLLABLES	
161.	57	***	b __ gi __ __ ing
162.	59	***	c __ __ i __ tee
163.	60	***	crit __ __ __ __
164.	62	**	d __ __ __ __ rent
165.	63	***	disa __ __ __ r
166.	66	***	__ qu __ p __ __ __ t
167.	67	***	e __ ist __ __ __
168.	71	**	hin __ __ __ __
169.	75	***	in __ __ __ fe __ __
170.	75	***	int __ __ __ upt

	PAGE NUMBER	SYLLABLES	
171.	80	***	mini __ __ __ __
172.	83	***	prin __ __ __ __ l
173.	83	***	priv __ l __ __ __
174.	85	***	r __ li __ __ __ __ s
175.	87	***	sig __ __ __ __ __
176.	97	**	cons __ __ __ s
177.	103	**	k __ __ __ l __ __ e
178.	116	****	__ __ __ __ p __ n __
179.	137	****	av __ __ l __ __ __ __
180.	138	***	b __ s __ c __ __ __ __

It's a good idea to copy words you want to learn into your personal spelling bank and use them for learning four at a time and/or checking as described on pages 99–102.

Learning spellings

	PAGE NUMBER	SYLLABLES	
181.	161	****	_ _ _ di _ t _
182.	167	***	re _ y _ _ ng
183.	205	**	pro _ _ a _ _ _
184.	211	***	b _ _ t _ _ _
185.	212	****	_ _ mm _ n _ t _
186.	212	*****	c _ r _ o _ it _
187.	233	**	r _ _ _ b _ _ _ _
188.	241	**	th _ _ _ f _ _ _
189.	256	***	a _ _ _ _ d _ _ _
190.	262	***	_ _ p _ _ t _ _ t

	PAGE NUMBER	SYLLABLES	
191.	11	****	_ xa _ _ _ ra _ e
192.	31	****	a _ el _ r _ t _
193.	31	****	a _ _ ept _ _ _
194.	31	***	a _ _ _ e _ _ iv _
195.	37	****	espe _ _ _ _ _ y
196.	38	****	ex _ _ _ i _ _ _ t
197.	43	***	l _ _ _ ten _ _ _
198.	46	***	_ o _ _ ess _ n
199.	47	***	pr _ fe _ _ _ _ n
200.	53	*****	veg _ t _ r _ _ n

It's a good idea to copy words you want to learn into your personal spelling bank and use them for learning four at a time and/or checking as described on pages 99–102.

Learning spellings

PAGE	NUMBER	SYLLABLES		
201.	62	***	dic __ __ n __ __ __	
202.	63	***	disa __ __ __ nt	
203.	63	***	dis __ __ pl __ __ __	
204.	74	*****	__ __ d __ vid __ __	
205.	82	****	p __ __ tic __ l __ __	
206.	85	****	ridic __ l __ __ s	
207.	88	***	su __ __ i __ __ __ __ t	
208.	97	**	con __ __ __ __ __ ce	
209.	97	***	co __ __ __ spond	
210.	116	***	a __ __ __ mpl __ sh	

PAGE	NUMBER	SYLLABLES		
211.	122	***	g __ v __ __ n __ __ __ __	
212.	147	**	play __ __ __ __ t	
213.	153	***	a __ __ ear __ __ __ __	
214.	153	****	a __ __ e __ i __ t __	
215.	157	****	exp __ r __ __ __ __ __	
216.	158	***	__ __ __ qu __ __ t __ __	
217.	210	****	a __ __ umu __ __ __ __	
218.	228	***	d __ s __ st __ __ __	
219.	245	***	d __ __ er __ __ __ __ d	
220.	281	***	out __ __ __ __ __ __ s	

It's a good idea to copy words you want to learn into your personal spelling bank and use them for learning four at a time and/or checking as described on pages 99–102.

Learning spellings

PAGE NUMBER	SYLLABLES		
221.	1	*****	_ cc _ _ _ t _ _ _ y
222.	12	****	fas _ _ n _ _ ing
223.	23	****	pra _ t _ c _ l _ _
224.	38	****	expl _ n _ _ _ _
225.	46	****	prep _ r _ _ _ _
226.	48	***	r _ memb _ _ _ _
227.	73	****	ind _ p _ nd _ nt
228.	80	***	mis _ _ _ v _ _ _
229.	94	****	acc _ _ _ _ d _ t _
230.	96	****	comp _ ti _ _ _

PAGE NUMBER	SYLLABLES		
231.	97	****	cont _ ov _ _ _ _
232.	107	*****	o _ _ _ t _ n _ ty
233.	128	*****	pr _ nun _ _ _ _ ion
234.	135	*****	u _ ne _ _ _ _ ry
235.	137	***	_ _ qu _ _ nt _ _ ce
236.	146	***	m _ _ nt _ _ _ _ ce
237.	147	*****	o _ _ a _ _ _ _ _ ly
238.	155	****	_ _ ve _ _ _ nce
239.	161	*****	imm _ _ _ _ _ _ ly
240.	265	***	p _ f _ _ _ _ nce

It's a good idea to copy words you want to learn into your personal spelling bank and use them for learning four at a time and/or checking as described on pages 99–102.

Answers

PRACTICE WITH LONG VOWEL SOUNDS

PAGE 14

FOOD

1. toast	208	**6.** pastry	147	**11.** sweet	171	**16.** cream	155
2. ice-cream	183	**7.** savoury	149	**12.** rice	189	**17.** loaf	201
3. roll	206	**8.** muesli	217	**13.** oats	203	**18.** fruit	214
4. flavour	142	**9.** gravy	143	**14.** soup	221	**19.** plaice	147
5. cake	139	**10.** meat	164	**15.** cheese	155	**20.** tasty	151

IN THE COUNTRY

1. lake	145	**6.** stream	171	**11.** pool	219	**16.** drainage	140
2. field	158	**7.** wheat	174	**12.** rye	189	**17.** hay	144
3. acorn	137	**8.** oak	203	**13.** trees	172	**18.** leaves	163
4. root	220	**9.** toadstool	208	**14.** flies	181	**19.** spider	191
5. stone	207	**10.** bluebells	211	**15.** nightingale	187	**20.** snake	149

SPORT

1. team	172	**6.** crew	212	**11.** race	148	**16.** skiing	170
2. skating	149	**7.** rowing	206	**12.** climbing	178	**17.** glider	182
3. height	182	**8.** diving	179	**13.** player	147	**18.** bowler	195
4. fielder	158	**9.** boot	211	**14.** try	192	**19.** goal	199
5. snooker	221	**10.** rival	189	**15.** losing	216	**20.** rules	220

OCCUPATIONS

1. playwright	147	**6.** director	179	**11.** agent	137	**16.** poet	205
2. waiter	152	**7.** cleaner	155	**12.** labourer	145	**17.** dealer	156
3. salesman	149	**8.** librarian	185	**13.** student	221	**18.** jeweller	216
4. miner	186	**9.** programmer	205	**14.** newsagent	218	**19.** painter	147
5. preacher	166	**10.** fireman	181	**15.** pirate	188	**20.** leader	163

TRAVEL

1. railway	148	**6.** road	206	**11.** pony	205	**16.** plane	147
2. scooter	221	**7.** bicycle	177	**12.** flight	181	**17.** cruise	212
3. breakdown	138	**8.** timetable	192	**13.** train	151	**18.** driver	179
4. motorist	202	**9.** wheels	174	**14.** pilot	188	**19.** vehicle	173
5. ocean	203	**10.** route	220	**15.** detour	156	**20.** scenery	169

Answers

PRACTICE WITH SHORT VOWEL SOUNDS

PAGE 15

WILDLIFE

1. butterfly	116	6. vixen	91	11. winkle	92	16. thrush	133
2. moth	105	7. cub	118	12. cockle	96	17. dove	120
3. squirrel	89	8. otter	107	13. mussel	126	18. swan	112
4. badger	5	9. jellyfish	42	14. lobster	104	19. kestrel	42
5. fox	100	10. crab	8	15. sparrow	27	20. slug	130

HOSPITAL

1. ambulance	2	6. splint	88	11. health	40	16. drug	120
2. bandage	5	7. temperature	52	12. lung	125	17. tablet	28
3. injury	74	8. blood	116	13. oxygen	107	18. pill	82
4. fracture	13	9. vaccine	29	14. scalpel	26	19. medication	44
5. limb	79	10. stethoscope	51	15. unconscious	134	20. stomach	131

WINTER

1. frost	100	6. gloves	122	11. decorate	34	16. mistletoe	80
2. shiver	87	7. anorak	2	12. presents	47	17. berries	32
3. wintry	92	8. robin	110	13. tinsel	90	18. sledge	50
4. blizzard	58	9. Christmas	59	14. glisten	70	19. pantomime	22
5. slush	130	10. carolling	7	15. holly	102	20. January	18

HOLIDAYS

1. sand	25	6. suntan	132	11. tent	52	16. visit	91
2. bucket	117	7. cottage	97	12. caravan	7	17. exhibition	38
3. paddle	22	8. fishing	69	13. disco	62	18. restaurant	49
4. swimming	89	9. camping	7	14. shopping	111	19. customs	119
5. deckchair	34	10. rucksack	129	15. trip	90	20. luggage	125

GAMES AND PASTIMES

1. cricket	59	6. badminton	5	11. snap	26	16. rugby	129
2. chess	33	7. squash	111	12. dominoes	99	17. boxing	95
3. golf	101	8. netball	45	13. lotto	104	18. sledging	51
4. hockey	102	9. putting	128	14. skipping	88	19. stilts	88
5. tennis	52	10. jigsaws	77	15. football	121	20. juggling	124

Answers

PRACTICE WITH MIXED LONG AND SHORT VOWEL SOUNDS

PAGE 16

SCHOOL

1. cloakroom	196	6. lesson	43	11. lunch	125	16. copy	97
2. desk	34	7. bell	32	12. monitor	105	17. science	190
3. seat	169	8. break	138	13. prefect	166	18. mathematics	20
4. teacher	172	9. snack	26	14. writing	193	19. games	143
5. subject	131	10. queue	219	15. notes	202	20. music	217

DRINKS

1. smoothie	221	6. chocolate	96	11. shandy	26	16. brandy	6
2. lemonade	43	7. grapefruit	143	12. beer	154	17. alcoholic	2
3. milk	80	8. juice	216	13. cider	178	18. fizzy	69
4. coffee	96	9. wine	193	14. scotch	111	19. tonic	113
5. tea	172	10. punch	128	15. whisky	92	20. soda	207

GUY FAWKES

1. evening	157	6. sticks	88	11. heat	160	16. banger	5
2. clothes	196	7. matches	21	12. bake	138	17. fuse	214
3. fire	181	8. light	185	13. sausages	111	18. taper	151
4. wood	136	9. flame	142	14. fireworks	181	19. glow	199
5. paper	147	10. crackle	9	15. colours	118	20. embers	36

MOUNTAINS

1. peak	166	6. huge	215	11. precipice	46	16. crag	8
2. massive	20	7. summit	132	12. sheer	170	17. crevice	33
3. rugged	129	8. ridge	84	13. edge	36	18. trail	151
4. boulders	195	9. slope	207	14. torrent	113	19. scramble	26
5. pinnacle	82	10. avalanche	3	15. rocky	110	20. gully	122

THE RAILWAY STATION

1. ticket	90	6. platform	23	11. diesel	156	16. sleeper	170
2. office	106	7. notice	202	12. carriage	8	17. signal	87
3. clock	96	8. timetable	192	13. train	151	18. buffers	117
4. case	139	9. kiosk	162	14. rails	148	19. bridge	57
5. trolley	113	10. engine	36	15. whistle	92	20. taxi	28

© David Moseley and Gwyn Singleton 2015 | *ACE Spelling Activities* | LDA | Permission to photocopy

Answers

PAGE 17

FUN

1. smile	190	6. skipping	88	11. acting	1	16. chuckling	118
2. party	233	7. kissing	78	12. painting	147	17. giggling	70
3. happy	16	8. hugging	123	13. joke	201	18. merry	44
4. mirth	249	9. clown	277	14. tease	172	19. cartoon	227
5. joyful	272	10. tumbling	133	15. tickle	90	20. comic	96

ON THE FARM

1. tractor	28	6. yard	235	11. corn	258	16. cattle	8
2. plough	282	7. orchard	264	12. barley	226	17. bullock	117
3. furrow	121	8. hedgerow	40	13. crop	96	18. sheep	170
4. fertiliser	246	9. harvest	230	14. dairy	237	19. goose	214
5. slurry	130	10. grain	143	15. herd	247	20. turkey	253

WATER

1. waves	152	6. calm	227	11. whirlpool	255	16. trickle	90
2. splash	26	7. smooth	221	12. current	119	17. pour	265
3. spray	149	8. tranquil	29	13. squirt	252	18. still	88
4. choppy	96	9. river	86	14. jet	42	19. sparkling	234
5. rough	129	10. flow	198	15. fountain	279	20. pure	219

FLOWERS

1. snowdrop	207	6. tulip	222	11. lily	79	16. foxglove	100
2. cowslip	277	7. marigold	20	12. lavender	19	17. thistle	90
3. hyacinth	182	8. pansy	22	13. heather	40	18. poppy	108
4. crocus	196	9. carnation	227	14. gorse	261	19. buttercup	116
5. daffodil	10	10. orchid	264	15. broom	211	20. daisy	140

TREES

1. chestnut	33	6. birch	243	11. fir	246	16. oak	203
2. beech	154	7. ash	1	12. pine	188	17. olive	106
3. willow	92	8. palm	233	13. spruce	221	18. hazel	144
4. sycamore	88	9. holly	102	14. yew	224	19. mulberry	126
5. poplar	108	10. larch	231	15. bay	138	20. maple	146

SPELLINGS FOR SOUNDS

PAGE 18	PAGE 20	PAGE 22	PAGE 24
1. axle	1. again	1. bridge	1. bomb
2. banned	2. bench	2. build	2. conquer
3. camel	3. cellar	3. Christmas	3. dolphin
4. carrot	4. chemist	4. crystal	4. glossy
5. chapter	5. debt	5. filthy	5. knocked
6. expand	6. exit	6. hymn	6. knot
7. fragile	7. friend	7. kitchen	7. lobster
8. accident	8. guest	8. liquid	8. mosque
9. gamble	9. leisure	9. minute	9. novel
10. hammock	10. lesson	10. pistol	10. olive
11. language	11. meadow	11. busy	11. omelette
12. manner	12. pedal	12. ring	12. profit
13. married	13. petrol	13. symbols	13. quarry
14. panda	14. refuge	14. villain	14. squash
15. scratch	15. thread	15. witch	15. watt

PAGE 26	PAGE 28	PAGE 30	PAGE 32
1. among	1. ache	1. appear	1. biceps
2. blush	2. ancient	2. beetle	2. bridle
3. pudding	3. break	3. creak	3. buyer
4. currant	4. cradle	4. deer	4. cyclist
5. enough	5. exhale	5. deceive	5. dilute
6. gloves	6. famous	6. eager	6. dye
7. pushchair	7. gait	7. equal	7. enquire
8. wolves	8. grate	8. frequent	8. guidance
9. plum	9. hazy	9. keyhole	9. idol
10. nun	10. jail	10. leased	10. lightning
11. rubbish	11. laid	11. meter	11. might
12. skull	12. mail	12. needle	12. pylon
13. some	13. mistake	13. peace	13. tide
14. troubles	14. tray	14. queasy	14. tire
15. upstairs	15. weight	15. seize	15. vibrate

Answers

PAGE 34	PAGE 36	PAGE 38	PAGE 40
1. bold	1. amuse	1. arc	1. aware
2. crowbar	2. beauty	2. barley	2. bare
3. dough	3. bruise	3. carpet	3. barely
4. frozen	4. choose	4. carton	4. careless
5. glow	5. cruise	5. catarrh	5. daring
6. grown-up	6. dew	6. farther	6. fare
7. loan	7. Europe	7. guitar	7. farewell
8. moan	8. gloomy	8. harpoon	8. hare
9. ocean	9. hooves	9. harvest	9. parent
10. poach	10. juice	10. heart	10. prepare
11. rows	11. new	11. lager	11. repair
12. snowdrop	12. nuisance	12. parcel	12. scary
13. sole	13. pollute	13. scarf	13. stare
14. throne	14. funeral	14. sergeant	14. there
15. yolk	15. shoot	15. varnish	15. where

PAGE 42	PAGE 44	PAGE 46	PAGE 48
1. absurd	1. awful	1. avoid	1. allowed
2. alert	2. board	2. boiling	2. bough
3. birth	3. daughter	3. buoy	3. coward
4. burglar	4. force	4. choice	4. crowd
5. colonel	5. fortune	5. coin	5. drowsy
6. dirty	6. gorgeous	6. employ	6. flower
7. earn	7. haunt	7. foyer	7. foul
8. fur	8. hawk	8. hoist	8. hour
9. gurgle	9. mourning	9. joyful	9. mouth
10. journal	10. naughty	10. ointment	10. plough
11. murder	11. saucer	11. oyster	11. rounders
12. murmur	12. shore	12. poison	12. rowdy
13. perfume	13. stalk	13. rejoice	13. sprout
14. purchase	14. walk	14. soiled	14. thousand
15. world	15. war	15. toil	15. trowel

Answers

SPELLINGS FOR SOUNDS PUZZLES

PAGE 50

1. potato
2. complaint
3. fragrant
4. greyhound
5. daisy
6. raisin
7. playmate

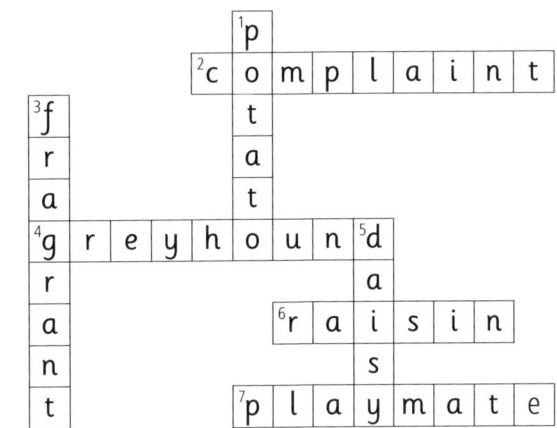

PAGE 51

1. skier
2. creeper
3. grieve
4. sphere
5. cedar
6. tweezers
7. machine

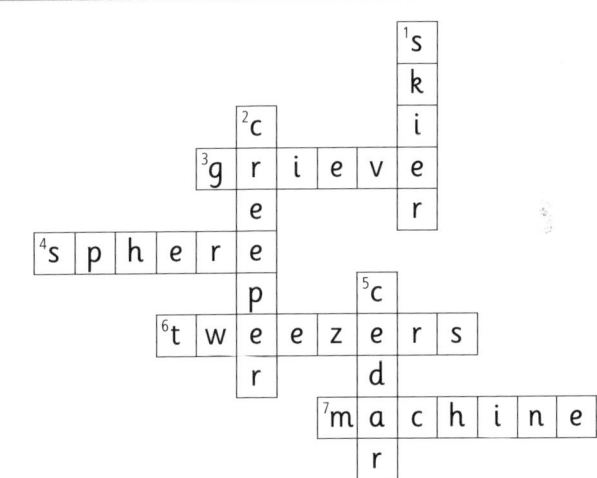

PAGE 52

1. strive
2. riot
3. private
4. frightened
5. nylon
6. migrate
7. oblige

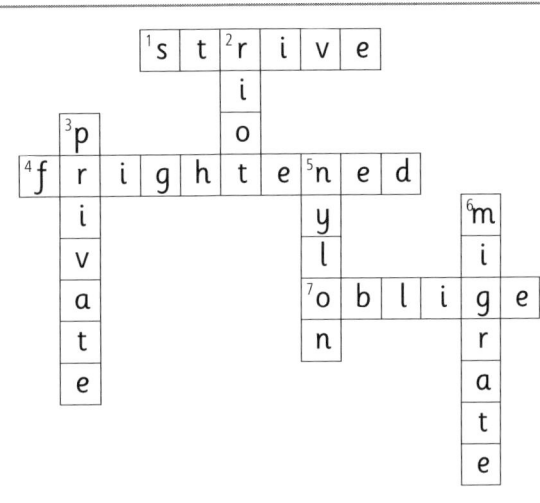

Answers

PAGE 53

1. blowlamp
2. photograph
3. doughnut
4. trophy
5. stolen
6. snowman
7. diploma

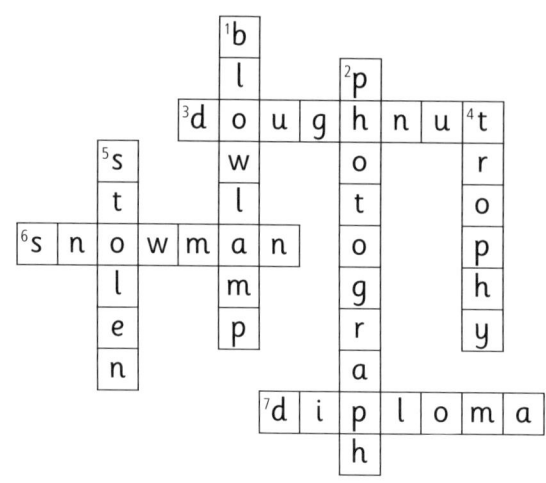

PAGE 54

1. rhubarb
2. sewage
3. hoover
4. futile
5. include
6. tomb
7. brute

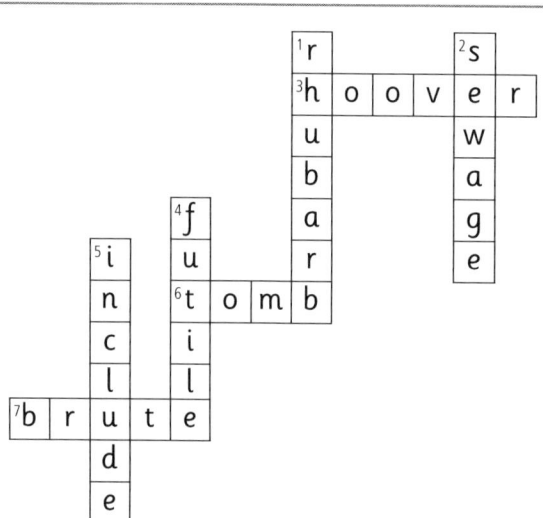

PAGE 55

1. sardine
2. departure
3. tarmac
4. scarlet
5. sharpen
6. charcoal
7. largest

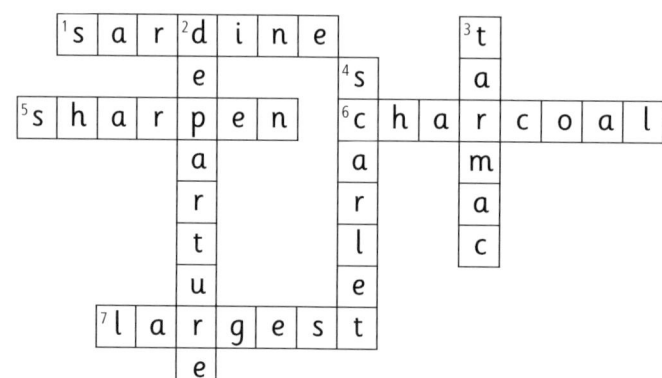

Answers

PAGE 56

1. scarce
2. warehouse
3. pharaoh
4. haircut
5. staircase
6. various
7. fairground

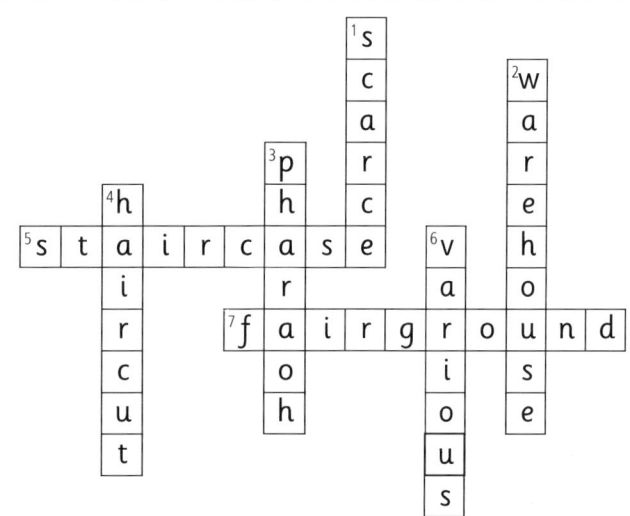

PAGE 57

1. thirsty
2. learning
3. vermin
4. nasturtium
5. suburban
6. world
7. purple

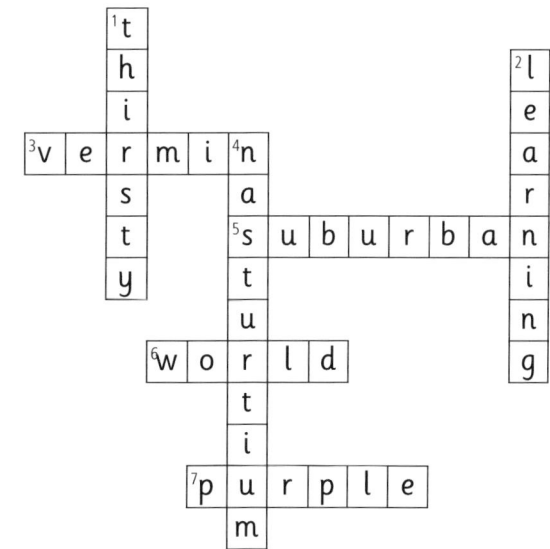

PAGE 58

1. dormouse
2. cautious
3. forecast
4. wharf
5. fourth
6. strawberry
7. wardrobe

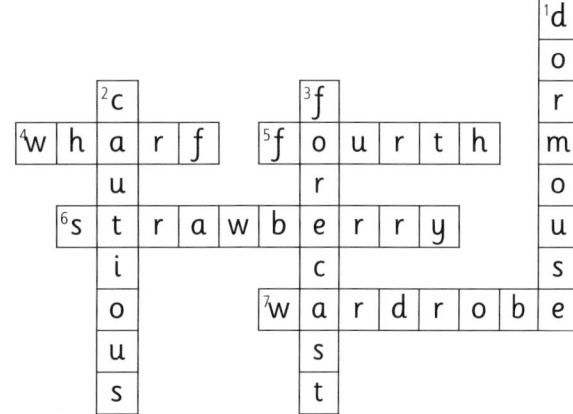

© David Moseley and Gwyn Singleton 2015 | *ACE Spelling Activities* | LDA | Permission to photocopy

Answers

PAGE 59

1. moisture
2. joinery
3. embroider
4. buoyant
5. poison
6. voyage
7. employment

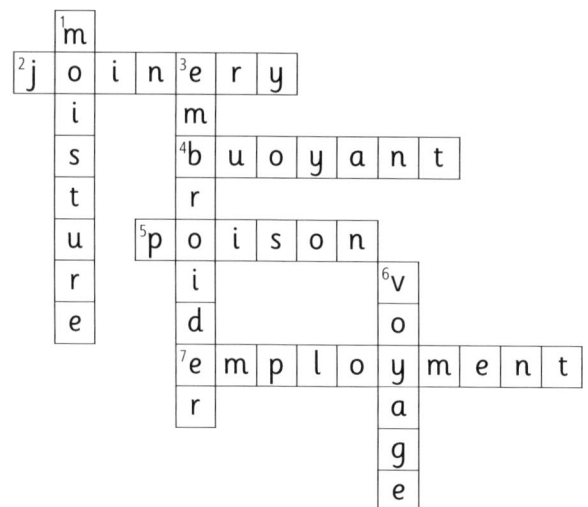

PAGE 60

1. howled
2. loudest
3. cowboy
4. voucher
5. powerful
6. trousers
7. showery

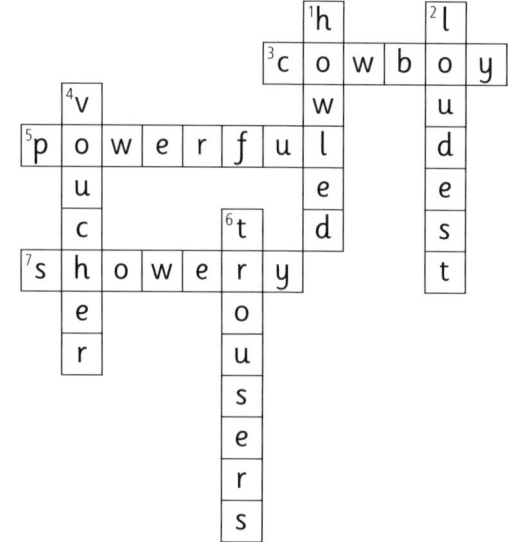

Answers

CAR REGISTRATION GAMES

PAGE 61

1. heavy
2. bacon
3. body
4. reward
5. woman
6. bracelet
7. ripen
8. secret

b	a	c	o	n	☆	☆	☆
w	o	m	a	n	☆	☆	☆
r	e	w	a	r	d	☆	☆
b	r	a	c	e	l	e	t
b	o	d	y	☆	☆	☆	☆
h	e	a	v	y	☆	☆	☆
s	e	c	r	e	t	☆	☆
r	i	p	e	n	☆	☆	☆

PAGE 62

1. ketchup
2. nightfall
3. ostrich
4. exhaust
5. fashion
6. whirlpool
7. reason
8. wicket

w	h	i	r	l	p	o	o	l
e	x	h	a	u	s	t	☆	☆
o	s	t	r	i	c	h	☆	☆
n	i	g	h	t	f	a	l	l
k	e	t	c	h	u	p	☆	☆
f	a	s	h	i	o	n	☆	☆
r	e	a	s	o	n	☆	☆	☆
w	i	c	k	e	t	☆	☆	☆

PAGE 63

1. leopard
2. dandruff
3. ocean
4. gorgeous
5. jiffy
6. ruby
7. reindeer
8. dungeon

r	e	i	n	d	e	e	r
r	u	b	y	☆	☆	☆	☆
d	u	n	g	e	o	n	☆
g	o	r	g	e	o	u	s
o	c	e	a	n	☆	☆	☆
j	i	f	f	y	☆	☆	☆
d	a	n	d	r	u	f	f
l	e	o	p	a	r	d	☆

Answers

TRICKY WORD ENDINGS

PAGE 64

1. jailer
2. motor
3. lever
4. liar
5. donor
6. pillar

Additional words:
  farmer
  voter
  razor
  mower

PAGE 65

1. harden
2. toughen
3. cousin
4. bacon
5. blacken
6. talon

Additional words:
  woman
  season
  deepen
  rotten

PAGE 66

1. nation
2. occupation
3. collision
4. session
5. motion
6. passion
7. magician
8. abbreviation
9. solution
10. optician

Additional words:
potion
vexation
lotion

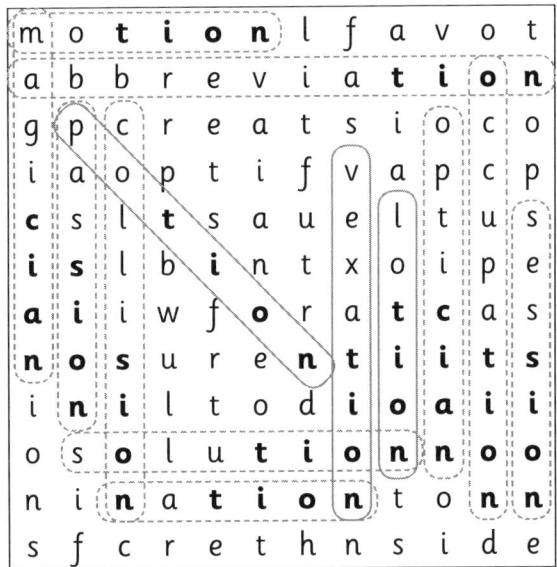

PAGE 67

1. discovery
2. nursery
3. satisfactory
4. extraordinary
5. recovery
6. complimentary
7. mastery
8. history
9. showery
10. victory

Additional words:
embroidery
every
mystery
ordinary
rectory

Answers

DOUBLES OR SINGLES

PAGE 68
1. manner
2. pepper
3. pilot
4. scooter
5. bullet
6. written
7. hammer
8. lapel
9. butter
10. totem

PAGE 69
1. lettuce
2. status
3. annoy
4. toilet
5. liner
6. drummer
7. super
8. lemon
9. illness
10. halo

Answers

FIND THE MIDDLE SYLLABLE

PAGE 70
1. parachute
2. entangled
3. bachelor
4. mascara
5. valiant
6. tapestry
7. javelin
8. battleship
9. subtraction
10. advertise
11. abandon
12. handkerchief
13. angrily
14. animals
15. familiar

PAGE 71
1. inspector
2. complexion
3. skeleton
4. wellington
5. terrify
6. delicate
7. merriment
8. recipe
9. penalty
10. venison
11. restaurant
12. flexible
13. offensive
14. pessimist
15. Celsius

PAGE 72
1. brigadier
2. flamingo
3. exquisite
4. neglectful
5. sinister
6. rickety
7. tributary
8. vanilla
9. intention
10. revolver
11. continue
12. decision
13. division
14. discussion
15. difficult

PAGE 73
1. bronchitis
2. corridor
3. solitude
4. volunteer
5. tomahawk
6. hospital
7. gossiping
8. mosquito
9. astonished
10. contradict
11. monument
12. probably
13. properly
14. doggedly
15. colossal

PAGE 74
1. buffalo
2. footballer
3. cookery
4. wonderful
5. bumblebee
6. customer
7. bulletin
8. multiply
9. unconscious
10. wondering
11. bungalow
12. another
13. discourage
14. sultana
15. suddenly

PAGE 75
1. patiently
2. masonry
3. stationery
4. amazement
5. narrator
6. labelling
7. mistaken
8. neighbourhood
9. dangerous
10. tablespoon
11. shakily
12. impatient
13. vacation
14. frustration
15. stadium

PAGE 76
1. preceded
2. achievement
3. vehement
4. weariness
5. vehicle
6. tedious
7. previous
8. cereal
9. reassure
10. equally
11. conceited
12. scenery
13. lenient
14. sincerely
15. media

PAGE 77
1. exciting
2. migrating
3. triangle
4. xylophone
5. library
6. assignment
7. gigantic
8. horizon
9. livelihood
10. triumphant
11. ivory
12. bribery
13. financial
14. designer
15. survivor

Answers

PAGE 78	PAGE 79	PAGE 80
1. aroma	1. museum	1. spectacles
2. immobile	2. hooligan	2. exhausted
3. ownership	3. duplicate	3. vigorous
4. devotion	4. tubular	4. architect
5. groceries	5. amusement	5. lemonade
6. foliage	6. jubilee	6. bicycle
7. atrocious	7. commuter	7. marvellous
8. sociable	8. lubricate	8. gorilla
9. loneliness	9. ruinous	9. burglary
10. emotion	10. pneumatic	10. foreigner
11. odious	11. beautiful	11. orchestra
12. coconut	12. intruder	12. mosaic
13. ferocious	13. secluded	13. certainly
14. jovial	14. fugitive	14. mountainous
15. viola	15. luminous	15. appointment

Answers

FIND THE TWO MIDDLE SYLLABLES

PAGE 81	PAGE 82
1. victorious	1. notorious
2. impossible	2. coronation
3. population	3. accumulate
4. environment	4. temporary
5. development	5. proprietor
6. superstition	6. economies
7. photography	7. communicate
8. identical	8. vegetation
9. ridiculous	9. hilarious
10. favourable	10. astronomy
11. kilometre	11. supermarket
12. minority	12. carnivorous
13. embarrassing	13. tonsillitis
14. memorial	14. peculiar
15. spontaneous	15. horizontal

Answers

WORDS WITHIN WORDS

PAGE 83

The following answers are those which can be found in the *ACE Spelling Dictionary*. Other correct answers (e.g. thundershower) are, of course, acceptable.

1.	safe	safeguard
2.	care	carefree, careful, carefully, carelessly, caretaker
3.	fit	fitting, fitness
4.	fun	funfair, funnier, funnily
5.	rock	rockery, rockier, rockiest
6.	thunder	thunderbolt, thunderclap, thundercloud, thunderous, thunderstorm, thunderstruck
7.	net	netball, netted, netware, network, networking
8.	rain	rainbow, raincoat, rainfall, rainier, raining
9.	down	downcast, downfall, downhill, downland, download, downright, downstairs, downstream, downturn, downward
10.	earth	earthenware, earthquake, earthworm
11.	shop	shopkeeper, shoplift, shopping
12.	slip	slipper, slippered, slippery, slipping, slipstone
13.	foot	football, foothill, foothold, footpath
14.	bright	brightened, brightest, brightness
15.	some	somebody, somehow, someone, something, sometime, somewhat, somewhere

Answers

PAGE 84

The following answers are those which can be found in the *ACE Spelling Dictionary*. Other correct answers (e.g. personable) are, of course, acceptable.

1.	cent	centenary, centigrade, centipede, centrifugal, centrifugally, centurion, century
2.	dirt	dirtied, dirtier, dirties, dirtiest
3.	cheer	cheerful, cheering
4.	sign	signpost
5.	whole	wholegrain, wholehearted, wholeheartedly, wholesale, wholesome
6.	dread	dreadful, dreadfully
7.	infect	infection, infectious
8.	person	personality, personally, personnel
9.	favour	favourable, favourably, favouritism
10.	govern	government, governmental
11.	school	schoolboy, schoolgirl, schoolmaster, schoolmistress, schoolteacher
12.	greed	greedier, greediest, greedily
13.	time	timeless, timescale, timetable, timetabling
14.	point	pointedly, pointing, pointless
15.	agree	agreement

Answers

FIND THE BASEWORD OR ROOT

PAGE 85

1.	a	polite
2.	b	explode
3.	b	mine
4.	a	plant
5.	a	cheat
6.	b	scorn
7.	b	globe
8.	b	rely
9.	a	simple
10.	b	fiction

PAGE 86

1.	b	mortal
2.	a	liberate
3.	a	joy
4.	b	optic
5.	b	navigate
6.	a	view
7.	b	stream
8.	b	employ
9.	a	less
10.	b	accept

Answers

INTRODUCING THE PARTS OF SPEECH

PAGE 87
1. brigade
2. blaze
3. bale
4. bracelet

1. hostess
2. hotel
3. home
4. hosepipe

1. drum
2. dummy
3. dungarees
4. dove

1. furniture
2. fern
3. furnace
4. fertiliser

PAGE 88
1. meat
2. machine
3. measles
4. meal

1. square
2. scarecrow
3. share
4. staircase

1. crucifix
2. computer
3. cucumber
4. clue

1. cloud
2. councillor
3. crown
4. couch

PAGE 89
1. flavoured
2. framed
3. faded
4. forgave

1. peck
2. pestered
3. pedalling
4. pressed

1. counting
2. cowered
3. crown
4. crowded

1. trudging
2. thumped
3. tunnelling
4. touch

PAGE 90
1. searching
2. stirred
3. surging
4. swerve

1. tie
2. timetabled
3. tried
4. time

1. besieged
2. breed
3. breathe
4. beat

1. chopping
2. cross
3. comment
4. complicate

PAGE 91
1. polite
2. private
3. psychic
4. primary

1. ravenous
2. ramshackle
3. ragged
4. Random

1. toxic
2. tropical
3. toffee
4. throbbing

1. naughty
2. normal
3. nautical
4. northern **or** north-east

PAGE 92
1. Understandably
2. unconventionally
3. undoubtedly
4. underfoot

1. shyly
2. scientifically
3. silently
4. Surprisingly

1. temporarily
2. technically
3. torrentially
4. terribly

1. tactfully
2. tragically
3. tyrannically
4. thankfully

Answers

SLIPPERY CHARACTERS

PAGES 109–110
1. equip
2. women
3. often
4. money
5. eight
6. reign
7. chief
8. weird
9. guide
10. lying
11. rhyme
12. group
13. scary
14. early
15. earth
16. heard
17. learn
18. occur
19. awful
20. forty
21. actual
22. harass
23. vacuum
24. breath
25. centre
26. energy
27. except
28. length
29. pigeon
30. rhythm
31. symbol
32. system
33. occupy
34. luxury
35. muscle
36. eighth
37. exceed
38. genius
39. recent
40. arrive

PAGES 111–112
41. decide
42. island
43. though
44. future
45. pursue
46. usable
47. answer
48. arctic
49. circle
50. fourth
51. absence
52. amateur
53. attract
54. average
55. grammar
56. imagine
57. natural
58. perhaps
59. tragedy
60. address
61. century
62. develop
63. mention
64. possess
65. regular
66. several
67. special
68. suggest
69. twelfth
70. weather
71. similar
72. vicious
73. foreign
74. popular
75. promise
76. strange
77. achieve
78. deceive
79. disease
80. extreme

PAGES 113–114
81. receipt
82. sincere
83. thieves
84. hygiene
85. licence
86. variety
87. suppose
88. through
89. article
90. bargain
91. bizarre
92. pharaoh
93. burglar
94. certain
95. further
96. purpose
97. awkward
98. forward
99. quarter
100. thought
101. accident
102. actually
103. apparent
104. attached
105. category
106. marriage
107. sandwich
108. cemetery
109. definite
110. exercise
111. February
112. medicine
113. pleasant
114. pressure
115. question
116. relevant
117. sentence
118. separate
119. strength
120. addition

PAGES 115–116
121. business
122. consider
123. equipped
124. horrific
125. increase
126. interest
127. mischief
128. misspell
129. omission
130. physical
131. position
132. broccoli
133. opposite
134. possible
135. thorough
136. grateful
137. occasion
138. straight
139. completely
140. material
141. describe
142. guidance
143. surprise
144. shoulder
145. although
146. humorous
147. barbecue
148. sergeant
149. tomatoes
150. forwards
151. embarrass
152. guarantee
153. sacrifice
154. desperate
155. excellent
156. necessary
157. prejudice
158. recognise
159. recommend
160. vegetable

Answers

PAGES 117–118

161. beginning
162. committee
163. criticise
164. different
165. disappear
166. equipment
167. existence
168. hindrance
169. interfere
170. interrupt
171. miniature
172. principal
173. privilege
174. religious
175. signature
176. conscious
177. knowledge
178. accompany
179. available
180. basically
181. immediate
182. recycling
183. programme
184. beautiful
185. community
186. curiosity
187. raspberry
188. therefore
189. according
190. important
191. exaggerate
192. accelerate
193. acceptable
194. aggressive
195. especially
196. experiment
197. lieutenant
198. possession
199. profession
200. vegetarian

PAGES 119–120

201. dictionary
202. disappoint
203. discipline
204. individual
205. particular
206. ridiculous
207. sufficient
208. conscience
209. correspond
210. accomplish
211. government
212. playwright
213. appearance
214. appreciate
215. experience
216. frequently
217. accumulate
218. disastrous
219. determined
220. outrageous
221. accidentally
222. fascinating
223. practically
224. explanation
225. preparation
226. remembrance
227. independent
228. mischievous
229. accommodate
230. competition
231. controversy
232. opportunity
233. pronunciation
234. unnecessary
235. acquaintance
236. maintenance
237. occasionally
238. convenience
239. immediately
240. performance

IMPROVING PERFORMANCE IN PRIMARY SCHOOLS

Easy-to-use proformas for whole-school development and self-evaluation

Kevin Bullock

© Kevin Bullock 2005

Original edition published by pfp, ISBN 0-904677-06-1
New edition, published by Optimus Education, 2007, ISBN 978-1-905538-41-6

All rights reserved. No part of this publication may be reproduced, stored in a retrieval system, or transmitted in any form or by any means, electronic, mechanical, photocopying, recording or otherwise without the permission of the publisher.

Applications for reproduction should be made in writing to
Optimus Education, 33-41 Dallington Street, London EC1V 0BB.

The information contained in this publication is believed to be correct at the time of going to press. Whilst care has been taken to ensure that the information is accurate, the publisher can accept no responsibility for any errors or omissions or for changes to the details given.

A CIP catalogue record for this book is available from the British Library.

Printed in England by:
Piggott Black Bear
The Paddocks
Cherry Hinton Road
Cambridge CB1 8DH
Tel: 01223 424571

Designed by:
Character Design
Highridge
Lower Wrigglebrook Lane
Kingsthorne
Hereford HR2 8AW
Tel: 01981 541154

Published by Optimus Education, a trading name of Optimus Professional Publishing Ltd, Registered Office 33-41 Dallington Street, London EC1V 0BB. Registered in England and Wales. Registered no. 05791519.

IMPROVING PERFORMANCE IN PRIMARY SCHOOLS

Easy-to-use proformas for whole-school development and self-evaluation

Kevin Bullock

Contents

Foreword 1

Getting to know the proformas 2

Sample proformas 3

Q&A 13

Introducing the proformas 15

Using the proformas 16

Managing the proformas 19

At a glance – Overview of proformas 20

Proforma tracking sheet 21

Step by step through the proformas 23

Section 1:
Proformas that monitor pupils' work and progress 23

Section 2:
Proformas that assist subject coordinators in their role .. 24

Section 3:
Proformas that assist with whole-school strategic planning 24

Section 4:
Proformas that assist with collating performance information 25

Proformas 1-9

Monitoring pupils' work and progress 27

Proforma 1: Monitoring and presenting pupils' work 28

Proforma 2: Monitoring basic skills with inclusivity in mind 30

Proforma 3: Whole-school monitoring 32

Proforma 4: Work sampling 34

Proforma 5: Subject report evaluation sheet 36

Proforma 6: Class survey 38

Proforma 7: Expectation sheet 40

Proforma 8: Attitude/progress sheet 42

Proforma 9: SATs predictions 44

Proformas 10-14

Assisting the subject coordinators in their role **47**

Proforma 10: Subject coordinators' checklist 48

Proforma 11: Subject coordinators' summary of monitoring......... 50

Proforma 12: Improving standards 52

Proforma 13: Self-appraisal for subject coordinators............... 54

Proforma 14: My personal development planning sheet............ 56

Proformas 15-20

Whole-school strategic planning **59**

Proforma 15: Strategies for monitoring educational standards....... 60

Proforma 16: Subject priorities 62

Proforma 17: Teacher appraisal/monitoring...................... 64

Proforma 18: Teaching and learning observations................. 66

Proforma 19: Governing body 68

Proforma 20: School development 70

Proformas 21-24

Collating performance information **73**

Proformas 21 and 22: Prompting sentences...................... 74

Proforma 23: Continuous professional development for teachers 76

Proforma 24: Summary of CPD for individual teachers 78

Proformas 25-27

Performance management **82**

Proforma 25: The review meeting 83

Proforma 26: The planning statement/s 84

Proforma 27: The objectives................................... 85

Further reading **86**

Foreword

The emphasis on modern school inspection is embedded in self-evaluation.

> *Ofsted believes that schools are best placed to recognise their own strengths and weaknesses. This is why we are introducing a new inspection system which puts more onus on a school to be proactive and demonstrate to inspectors that it can not only diagnose where its strengths and weaknesses are, but more crucially, do something about improving and developing them.*
>
> (**www.ofsted.gov.uk/ofsteddirect** re: Self-evaluation and the self-evaluation form)

The proformas in this pack encourage **self-evaluation** – at **all** levels. As headteacher, you will be able to collate, through your staff, a wealth of robust self-evaluation information. Your teaching staff will have an easy-to-use process for evaluating their own teaching, and their pupils' learning, both as class teachers and as subject coordinators. All staff members will have a process for evaluating their own professional development. Governors and other stakeholders can contribute to the information you have about the school, by following the key questions in the proformas.

The proformas are designed to encourage **curriculum leadership** at all levels – a key Ofsted focus, and **continuous professional development** for all teachers – a major part of the government's *Excellence and Enjoyment* initiative.

The information you will gather when using these proformas will form a powerful tool in future Ofsted inspections, but more importantly, in your ongoing school improvement. This pack provides a framework that penetrates to the core of **teaching and learning**, enabling you, along with your school management team and your teachers, to focus more clearly on the pertinent issues:

Standards **A**chievement **L**earning **T**eaching

– the **SALT** of education.

The proformas are designed so that each aspect of information gathered can be fed back into whole-school development plans with ease. They provide a simple trail from class teaching to whole-school improvement and back again. The procedures are fast, robust and accurate. You can exchange the pastime of stumbling through stifling policies for directing and driving streamlined proformas. The valuable time saved in meetings, staff appraisals and school improvement reports will allow you space and energy to focus on the vision and direction of your school.

Throughout this pack the main aim is to keep **The Main Aim** as the main aim: in other words to allow you to concentrate on improving the teaching and learning in your school.

The term 'subject coordinator' has been used throughout the proformas – you can substitute this for 'subject leader', 'line manager' or whatever term is preferred in your school.

Getting to know the proformas

The proformas come in two styles:
- some provide advice for staff as they undertake evaluation procedures
- some are for completion.

All of them are accessible on the accompanying CD-Rom, so that you can modify them to suit your own school, add your school name, increase the size of boxes and so on.

Take time to familiarise yourself with these proformas before you try to introduce them to your staff. Pages 4 to 12 show some of the proformas filled in: look at these, alongside the master copies.

There are 27 proformas in all, covering a variety of activities and tasks. Some cover basic information while others are more complex. To a greater or lesser degree they are all interrelated, yet can be used in isolation when required.

The proformas are divided into five sections:
- monitoring pupils' work and progress (proformas 1 – 9)
- assisting the subject coordinators in their role (proformas 10 – 14)
- whole-school strategic planning (proformas 15 – 20)
- collating performance information (proformas 21 – 24)
- performance management.

Together these cover all aspects of school improvement work in a simple and straightforward format.

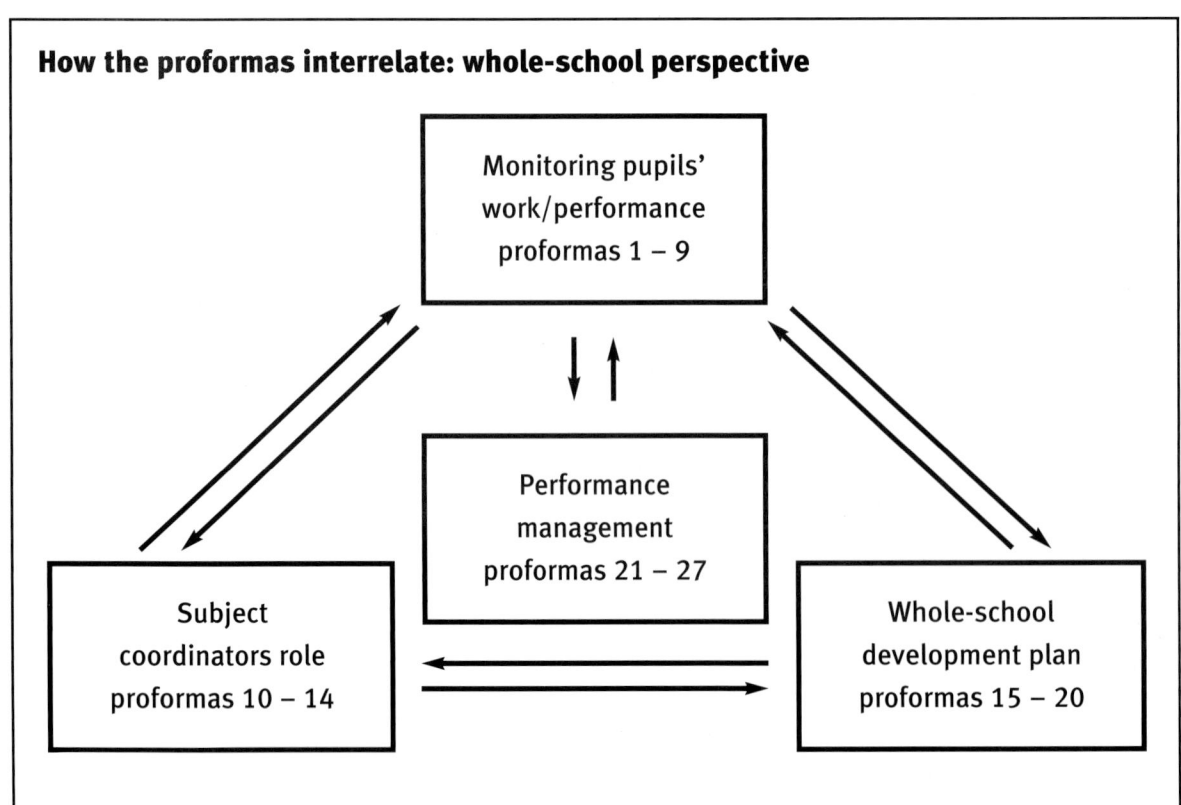

Accompanying each proforma is a guidance sheet. This provides information about:
- the intended objective/s
- links with the whole-school development cycle
- the key personnel for whom it is designed
- how it might contribute to whole-school improvement
- the next steps to take.

Read this information carefully, as it will help you to think about the most appropriate proforma to use to gather specific information about your school.

The important thing is to make the proformas work for you, with your staff and in your particular situation. This pack is versatile. It can be used to shape practice, highlight gaps and ensure a consistent approach in a variety of contexts. It is for you to decide how it can best be deployed in your school.

'All inspection findings must be rooted in evidence.
The most valuable and informative evidence is that obtained first hand...'

(Ofsted Handbook, 2003)

Ofsted highlights a hierarchical evidence base, of which the most valuable and informative are:
- observations/evidence of learning
- pupils' work/talking to pupils
- talking to staff/analysing performance indicators
- evaluating school processes in supporting/reinforcing the above.

The proformas are based on this premise.

Sample proformas

Please see overleaf for an illustration of how proformas can be cross-referenced.

'School development' proforma (20) is the starting point.

(20) School development

Priority
English SATs results in 2008

Target
To ensure we achieve 92% at L4 in the above test

Success criteria
92% is achieved in English in 2008

Task/s
Take stock of current standards — Expectation sheet, proforma 7
Transfer data onto SATs predictions sheet, proforma 9
Gain insight into pupil attitude/achievement perceptions via Attitude/progress sheet, proforma 8
Subject coordinator to complete improving standards report, based on above information — proforma 12
Line manager to support/direct subject coordinator via Personal development planning, proforma 14

Time scale	**Personnel**	**Resources**
Jan 07 – Summer 08	Subject coordinator Line manager Class teacher	Non-contact time
Monitoring and review	**Evaluation**	**Miscellaneous notes**
All monitoring info to be shared with teaching assistant. Monitoring meeting monthly with line manager.	To take place after results in 2008 are known — Teacher Subject coordinator Line manager Headteacher	Also use Work sampling proforma 4 In conjunction with Attitude/progress proforma 8

(7) Expectation sheet

Class ......*Mr Unknown*........................ Year ......*Year 5*..............................

Children working below their expected level in *English*

a) Slightly below
   Pupils   *1, 7, 9, 15, 21*   *(5 pupils)*

b) Below
   Pupils   *6, 7*   *(2 pupils)*

c) Substantially below
   Pupils   *4, 22*   *(2 pupils)*

Strategies to counter underachievement

Extra homework classes
Booster classes
Closer class monitoring of a + b pupils above

No. in class *30 (each child = 3.3%)*   **Usual time of lesson** *9:15 – 10:15*

Calculations

If A achieve   =   *21 + 5 = 26 pupils = 86%*

If B achieve   =   *21 + 7 = 28 = 92%*

If C achieve   =   *As there are a total of 9 pupils currently working below the expected level for this age we have 21 out of 30 who should achieve level 4.*

21 × 3.3% = 69%

To hit our target it is vital that both a + b pupils come up to expected level.

(9) SATs predictions

Name of teacher (current and previous) *Mrs ex-teacher, Mr Unknown*		
Year 2 SATs	**Year 6 SATs** ✓	**Results**
Percentage achieving Level ......4......... in		
Subject	**Best case scenario**	**Worst case scenario**
English ✓	*92%*	*69%*
Mathematics		
Science		

Related information	
No. IEPs	*3*
Previous: QCA optional SATs results	*See data with teacher but many pupils appear to have slipped back*
Relevant in-house test information	*See in-house reading tests data – again some slipped*
Teacher assessment/evidence	*Samples of work ready for analysis*
Baseline assessment or otherwise	*N/A*

Comments
The above best case scenario is dependent upon both slightly below and below expected level pupils achieving at expected level (see proforma 7).

(8) Attitude/progress sheet

Subject .... *English* .... Year ....

Date .... *Jan 21st* .... Name .... *Pupil X* ....

	Poor				Excellent
Confidence	1	(2)	3	4	5
Motivation	1	(2)	3	4	5
Listening	1	2	(3)	4	5
Communication	1	2	(3)	4	5

Effort	Achievement	Trend
A	A	**Improving**
B	B	
C	(C)	**Steady**
(D)	D	
E	E	**(More application needed)**

Comments

Pupil X is lacking both confidence and motivation, this in turn is having an effect on effort and achievement. As many of the pupils in this class scored low on motivation, I believe motivation is the key to improvement. It appears that the low confidence score is a result of low motivation and not the other way around.

(8) Attitude/progress sheet

Subject ....*English*........................ Year ....

Date ....*Jan 21st*........................ Name ....*Pupil Y*........................

	Poor				Excellent
Confidence	1	2	3	(4)	5
Motivation	1	(2)	3	4	5
Listening	1	2	(3)	4	5
Communication	1	2	(3)	4	5

Effort	Achievement	Trend
A	A	**Improving**
B	B	
(C)	C	**Steady**
D	(D)	
E	E	**(More application needed)**

Comments

Pupil Y is not the only pupil to score high on the confidence scale yet low on the motivation. I therefore believe motivation is a key factor in the lack of progress seen of late in this class.

(12) Improving standards

Improving standards in .... *English* .... (subject)

Brief report

Current standards/achievement (including specific cohorts of pupils year/key stage groups, etc.)

Current standards are low.

Progress has stalled.

Motivation appears to be a key factor in improving the situation.

Recent development work and how this has improved standards

N/A

Future development work and how this will improve standards

A sharp focus on teaching and learning in the classroom to ascertain why there is a lack of motivation.

In-depth chats to pupils to expand on why they're not motivated.

Monitoring meetings to evaluate progress on a monthly basis.

Robust work samples in English.

Extra booster classes.

Closer scrutiny of pupils' progress working below and slightly below expected level.

Other comments

Use 'My personal development planning sheet', proforma 14, to focus both on the subject coordinator's and class teacher's development.

(4) Work sampling

Three pupils from appropriate class/es working at above average standard, average standard, below average standard and any other relevant category bring work with them.

General questions might include

- What did you really enjoy doing?
- Why?
- Tell me about some of the things that you have learned.
- How do you think you are getting on in...?
- What didn't you enjoy doing?
- What things did you find most difficult?
- Why? Etc.

Focus also on specific pieces of work and ask them to tell you about how/why/when they did it, etc.

Other possible questions

Ask the pupil open questions that will give an insight into the apparent lack of motivation/confidence.

Get the pupil to talk about a piece of completed work of which they are really proud. What were the key factors that contributed to this success?

Ask questions that may shed some light on their peers' attitude towards class work (negative or otherwise).

Ask the pupil what would actually encourage them to work consistently harder.

(14) My personal development planning sheet — Class teacher

Priority

To motivate the significant number of 'switched-off' pupils.

Target

To ensure 92% of my class is working within the expected level for Year 4 pupils.

Success criteria

(see above) Are they?

Tasks

Modifying teaching and learning to motivate all pupils.

Modifying teaching and learning to improve pupil performance.

Time scale

July 08

Personnel to support me

Line manager

Resources I will need

To be discussed when line manager observes teaching and learning next week.

Peer support.

Monitoring review – how/who?

See proforma 12.

Evaluation

Miscellaneous notes

(14) My personal development planning sheet — Line manager

Priority

To support and direct class teacher as she modifies her teaching and learning in an attempt to re-motivate pupils.

Target

To ensure 92% of her class is working within the expected level for Year 4 pupils.

Success criteria

(see above) Are they?

Tasks

To support and direct teacher so that teaching and learning motivate all pupils.
To support and direct teacher in improving pupil performance.

Time scale

July 08

Personnel to support me

Headteacher

Resources I will need

To finalise after teaching and learning has been observed next week.

Monitoring review – how/who?

See proforma 12.

Evaluation

Miscellaneous notes

Q&A

What's the secret of the proformas' effectiveness?

Simply using tried-and-tested proformas to streamline communication, clarify key issues and focus directly on teaching and learning.

What if I have limited ICT skills?

There is no need to incorporate ICT with this pack. In fact, the sharing and passing on of handwritten proformas is as effective and seamless as many programs currently on the market.

What benefits will my school gain from using this pack?

- Every stakeholder in your school will feel they have a voice through completing one or more versions of the central 'School development' proforma (20), which identifies school priorities for improvement.
- The school will gain a broad view of priorities, taking account of the viewpoints of the different stakeholders.
- If all proformas are given out and returned within, say, 72 hours, you will have a framework for a comprehensive school development plan in just three days.
- The two whole-school development proformas can save hours of meetings and report writing.
- When the governor input grid has been incorporated into the sections of school development it can greatly enhance communication and problem solving.
- The school development proforma will revolutionise the way you keep abreast of school development, organisation and bureaucracy.

That may be the case, but won't prioritising the issues be a nightmare?

Prioritising will simply be about deciding into which of three piles you place the individual proformas: A, B or C.

A = Action (now)   B = Brewing   C = Coming up

The headteacher may make three tentative piles, but then through discussion with staff, governors and other stakeholders, the piles might be modified. The advantage to this procedure is that nothing is set in stone and you're not lumbered with an outdated document after a couple of months.

How do you incorporate the other proformas?

'School development' proforma (20) can be cross-referenced with any number of other proformas depending on the actual priority, and the amount of further information you require. Throughout this pack you will be guided to potential cross-referencing opportunities in the guidance sheets accompanying each proforma.

How will this help transform my leadership style?

This pack is a management tool. Using it will enable you to streamline the management of your school's development. These proformas will keep personnel on-task, leading them through the process of evaluating the performance of your school. With this taken care of, you will be released for the vital headship role of clear directional and strategic leadership. Remember, management is all about doing things right, while transformational leadership is all about doing the right things.

Effective leaders work on their indirect influence. They realise they can't split themselves into a dozen parts, but need to know that their staff are focused in their absence.

You can't be everywhere at once – but the proformas can!

Introducing the proformas

Once you are familiar with the proformas and how they can benefit your school, you need to decide how to share this with the rest of your staff and your governors.

Decide on a launch day, possibly a professional development day, and introduce your staff to the proformas and guidance.

- Photocopy the pack so that each proforma and its guidance notes are on a single A3 sheet.
- Provide each member of staff with a reference grid, with the proforma numbers and titles down the left hand side. Space on the right can be used for notes.

Allow time for staff to look through the material and familiarise themselves with the general layout. You could approach this in different ways:

- Whole packs could be spread out on tables and the staff could sit round in their key stage or year groups and discuss the proformas.
- Put one section of proformas, clearly labelled, on each of four large tables, one section per table, and allow staff to move round them in their own time.

You can then make a more formal presentation, introducing the proformas and how you intend that they should be used. It might be helpful if you have talked this through with your senior management team or other key staff first, so that they can support you in your presentation.

Introduce the system to your governors by explaining the process to them, explaining what is entailed and the benefits as you see them. Show them examples of the proformas and the accompanying guidance. Spend more time on the governors' proforma (19) and the school development proforma (20), explaining how these will improve your current approach to whole-school development.

There are alternative ways to use these proformas.

- **Cherry picking:** simply select a handful of proformas that would fill the gaps in your school's improvement programme and try them out. Modify them to fit the context of your own school and ask for feedback on their effectiveness. In short, select, trial and review a handful at a time.
- **Delegating choice:** this option gives your staff the initial responsibility for selecting the proformas to use within their own practice. As schools choose their own procedures for self-evaluation, so do individual teachers. Teachers are given copies of the whole pack and even granted professional development time to become familiar with aspects of it. They are then left to implement various categories into their own practice. It is likely that different individuals will have preferences for different proformas. After one or two terms organise whole-school feedback and evaluation to ascertain which proformas are the most popular and the most useful, and which are the least favoured. This in itself will give a good insight into school improvement issues.

Using the proformas

Like all planning, managing the performance of your school, in all its aspects, is a cyclical affair. To start the process you have to break into that cycle at some point. Once you have done this and set the ball rolling it will continue.

The whole pack centres on proforma 20, 'School development', so this is the point at which you could start the cycle for your school.

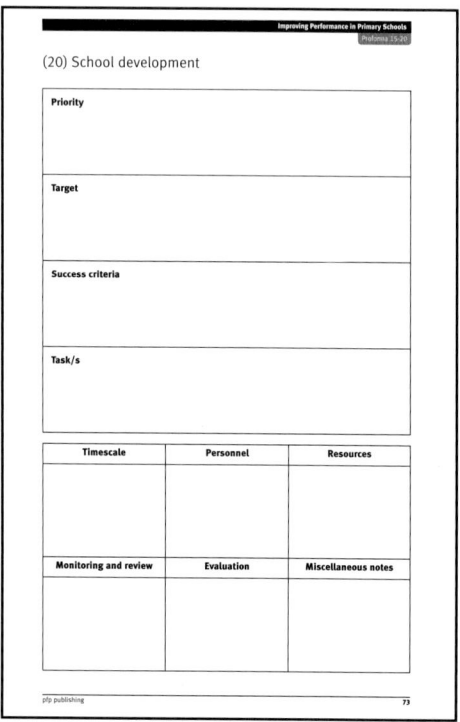

The headings will be familiar to you, even if the layout is new. This proforma is both the entry and the exit point for all your school development planning. The information gathered on all the other forms will eventually be reflected in it.

Distribute proforma 20

Make copies of proforma 20 and give one to each stakeholder: your staff (teachers, teaching assistants, PAs, cleaners, midday supervisors and so on), a representative sample of pupils and the governors. Ask them to fill in the first section, 'Priority', and return it to you within, say, 72 hours. Making this activity accessible to all empowers people, and the simplicity of the layout helps everyone to be able to contribute.

Alternatively, invite governors and other adult stakeholders to join teaching staff on a professional development day. Hand out copies of proforma 20 to each individual, ask them to complete the first section focusing on their own particular responsibilities. Spend the rest of the day deciding on the priorities and then detailing the tasks, etc. (see the following sections) and you can have your whole-school development plan completed in one day.

Once you have all the returned proformas, you will be able to finalise details and prioritise the issues.

Prioritise the priorities

Do this by setting up three piles.

Pile A	**Pile B**	**Pile C**
Action – now	Brewing	Coming up

These categories will represent issues that are of high, medium or low priority for your school at this point. The most challenging part of this process is deciding what goes into the school development plan (pile A), what goes into the reserve list (pile B) and what stops on its original pile (pile C).

Make three tentative piles yourself (having removed any duplicate priorities first), and then in discussion with staff, governors and other stakeholders, modify them. Decisions necessarily have to be context-based and evaluated by appropriate personnel.

The advantage of this procedure is that nothing is fixed, so it's easy to make changes now and 'unchange' them if necessary at some later date. You can easily re-categorise your priorities, up-grading or down-grading issues as school priorities change, as the result of the findings of an Ofsted inspection, as you realise through further self-evaluation that there is a more serious issue to be tackled, or in response to a changing government initiative. Because your priorities can be changed easily you will be willing to make those changes. There's nothing more annoying than having put it all into one document, taking hours of your time and the PA's time only to find that you need to make changes, and that means changing the whole thing – a daunting process that may cause you to react by ignoring it altogether. With this system you simply shuffle those papers and change the contents of your three piles.

Completing the proformas

If this is your first cycle you may need to pause at this point in order to collate more information, either by using other proformas from this pack or transferring information you already have. In future years you should have the information available.

The first section, 'Priority', will already be filled in.

The next two sections, 'Target' and 'Success criteria', will be familiar to you. 'Target' should be based on facts, not a notion or figure plucked from the air. There are proformas within the pack that will help you with this. 'Success criteria' should be measurable.

The fourth section is 'Tasks'; this section may include different information dependent upon the priority you have identified. It may be that there is a perceived problem or area for development identified in the priority section. You then need to collect the relevant data, in which case you will be listing the proformas to be used for this in the task section. Once you have this data you may decide that the priority as stated can in fact wait to be dealt with, and this proforma 20 can be moved to pile B or even pile C. It may be that the evidence proves the need for further action, in which case a new proforma 20 can be filled in. The task section will then include specific actions that staff will be taking to address the issue.

Alternatively, the priority may have been set because of the data you already have. In this case the proforma 20 will list the actions to be taken to address the issue.

Of course, a third option is that you will need a mixture of the two: proformas for further evidence and tasks, and maybe proformas to measure the level of success at the end of the process.

The remaining six boxes are self evident, but look at the sample proforma 20 on page 4 for more details.

Cross-referencing

If you look at the examples of completed proformas, pages 4 to 12, you will see how proformas can be cross-referenced.

In this particular example, the tasks are concerned primarily with completing other proformas to find out why results are low, and how they can be raised. So the relevant proformas are listed in the 'Tasks' section. (In the 'Personnel' section you could identify by number which proformas are to be completed by which section of personnel.) Having found out this information you may decide to complete another proforma 20, with the actions you need to take to address the issues raised by the information.

In some instances, the tasks will cover other actions that might be taken, and the proformas that hold the information leading to the identifying of the priority will then be listed in the monitoring and review section of proforma 20.

For other proformas there are suggestions for cross-referencing in the guide sheets.

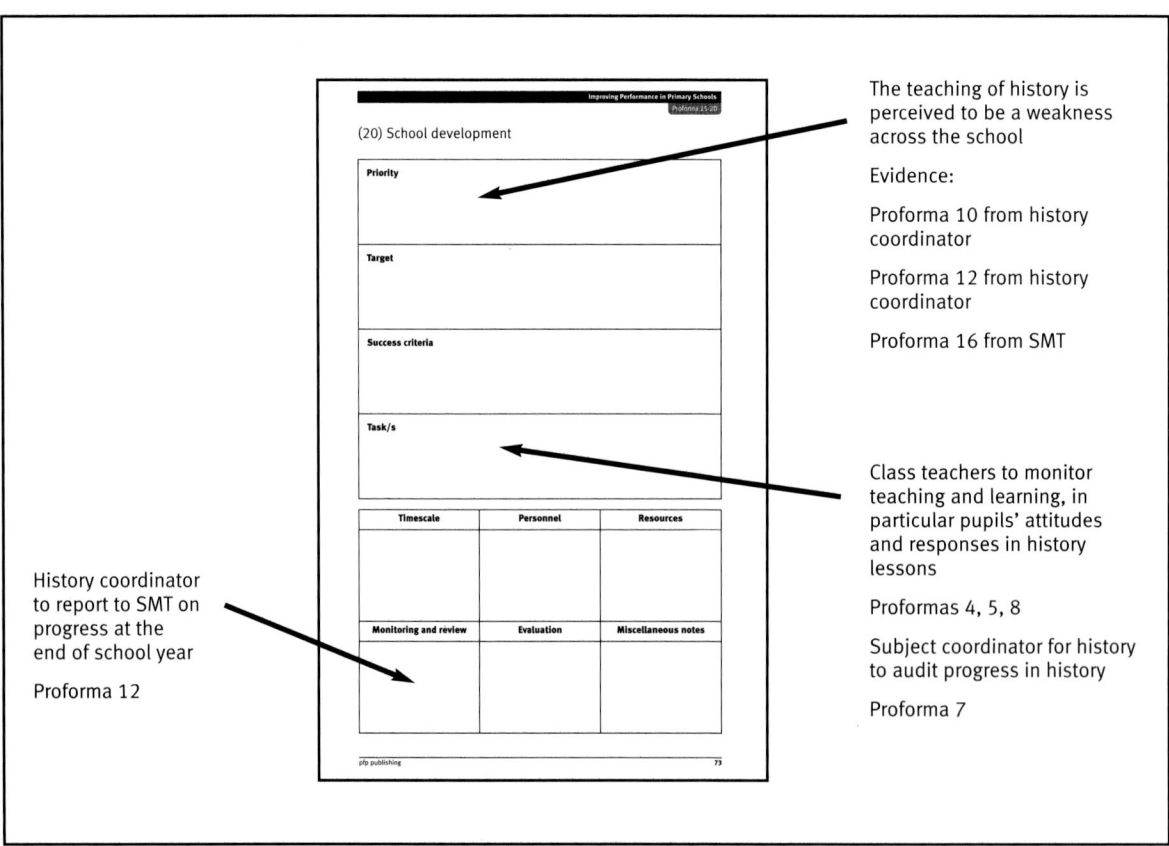

This is only one example of how varying proformas can link together to aid joined-up thinking. Any permutation is of course possible, depending on the priority and context.

Managing the proformas

Before you start to distribute proformas to your staff and stakeholders it is useful to spend some time thinking about how you will manage the many sheets of paper you could end up with. It is important that the information you store is accessible.

A key task is the storing and collating of information when copies of the proformas are returned to you. You need to set up a school improvement filing system covering the broad categories of this pack. Box files, drawer file units and suchlike are ideal. The proforma categorisation will be down to your own preference and reflect the context of your own school. Whatever system you decide upon, prepare it, or ask your PA to do this, before you introduce the pack to your staff. They need to know where everything is going to be stored.

Sorting out a storage system will help to clarify in your mind the way in which different proformas will impact on other proformas, on which ones will be used by other personnel within the school, which will be kept by class teachers or handed to senior staff and so on. Will you need a central system that all can access? If everything is kept in your office, who can access it? Which parts can be discarded and shredded once the information has been passed on or absorbed into another proforma?

Master copies of the proformas that you have decided class teachers will use, and their accompanying guidance sheets, should be prepared and stored for anyone to make their own copies as and when they need them.

Sometimes you will be distributing proformas to various members of your staff or your stakeholders. On page 21 you will find a sheet that you or a senior member of staff can use to track these. It will assist you to remember who is completing what, and by when. This is also evidence of the ongoing self-evaluation within your school, and as such is a document worth keeping.

You may need a perception shift within your school concerning whole-school improvement planning. Talking with your staff about the best ways to store and manage the data might lead naturally into this discussion. Discuss some of these statements with your staff and governors. It will help them to see the rationale of this new approach.

- The old system was neat because everything was in one easily-stored file.
- The information in the old file was quickly out of date.
- It was difficult to add to or change anything in the old file if a new priority arose.
- This material can be easily duplicated.
- Everyone can access the proformas and so contribute to the programme of managing improvement.
- Old style plans could slow down improvement due to their static and inaccessible nature.
- Information can be updated immediately.
- Information is easy to cross-reference.

Should files be the tail that wags the educational dog, or should continually improving practice dictate the rhythm and direction of the paperwork?

At a glance

Overview of proformas

1 Monitoring and presenting pupils' work 2 Monitoring basic skills with inclusivity in mind 3 Whole-school monitoring 4 Work sampling 5 Subject report evaluation sheet 6 Class survey 7 Expectation sheet 8 Attitude/progress sheet 9 SATs predictions sheet	**Monitoring pupils' work and progress** For itemised proformas see page 23
10 Subject coordinators' checklist 11 Subject coordinators' summary of monitoring 12 Improving standards 13 Self-appraisal for subject coordinators 14 My personal development planning sheet	**Assisting the subject coordinators in their role** For itemised proformas see page 24
15 Strategies for monitoring educational standards 16 Subject priorities 17 Teacher appraisal/monitoring 18 Teaching and learning observations 19 Governing body 20 School development	**Whole-school strategic planning** For itemised proformas see page 24 • Overall objectives • Monitoring • Teaching and learning • Whole-school development
21 Prompting sentences – Sheet 1 and 2 23 Continuous professional development for teachers 24 CPD for individual teachers	**Collating performance information** For itemised proformas see page 25
25 The review meeting 26 The planning statement 27 The objectives	**Performance management** For itemised proformas see page 26

Proforma tracking sheet

		Given to name/s	Date	Return date
Nos	Monitoring pupils' work			
	Subject coordinators' roles			
	Whole-school strategic planning			
	Performance management			

When Ofsted or other inspectors, or your governors want to know about your school improvement planning or your self-evaluation you can hand them a copy of the diagram on page 20: 'Overview of proformas'. They can then mark the ones which they will find useful and you can remove the appropriate files containing those specific proformas from your filing system. Completed forms will indicate any cross-referenced information and they can access this too if they so wish.

On the occasions that a written report on school development issues is required, information is simply lifted off the appropriate part of the proformas. The days of keeping a school development folder up to date and/or re-writing a new one every one, two or three years are over!

Step by step through the proformas

The following 27 proformas have been developed with both school inspection and school improvement in mind. They are tried and tested and have been effective in improving both standards and performance. In short they:

- focus on the important aspects of headship, teaching and learning
- support staff in self-assessment and further development so they are self-reliant with regard to future direction
- save valuable time thumbing through policy and handbooks – the proformas cover all areas of teaching and learning
- enhance joined-up thinking, teamwork and include all people at all levels
- revolutionise school development planning – no need for bulky folders which become outdated so quickly.

The proformas are divided into five sections

1. Monitoring pupils' work and progress
2. Assisting the subject coordinators in their role
3. Whole-school strategic planning
4. Collating performance information
4. Performance management

Section 1:

Proformas that monitor pupils' work and progress

Can be used by headteacher, subject coordinator and class teachers.

Overall objectives

1. To ensure focused monitoring and consistency in marking pupils' work.
   To remind teachers of some key learning information.
2. To clarify what we mean by inclusivity and raising questions to ensure that there is no under-achievement within the school.
3. To record the pupil groupings on a standardised form and highlight other key data about the grouping, so enabling an informative grouping profile to emerge.
4. To conduct effective work sampling by scrutinising above average, average and below average samples of pupils' work.
5. To obtain a written subject report from a pupil's perspective and additional personal information through interaction with the pupil.
6. To gauge the pupils' responses before the official letters and/or questionnaires are sent out at the time of the next Ofsted inspection.
7. To provide a class/year group expectation profile very quickly from which future target-setting data can be produced.
8. To provide an instant pupil profile snapshot covering effort, achievement and personal information.

9. To provide an instant snapshot (best and worst case scenarios) for SATs predictions in English, mathematics and science.

These proformas can be used individually or combined to inform the teacher, subject coordinator or headteacher on matters relating to the monitoring and progression of pupils' work. When the information has been recorded on the proformas they can be photocopied and handed on, or transferred to the appropriate subject coordinator proforma (see section 2) and fed into the overall school improvement plan. The subject coordinators' proformas can also assist the coordinator in identifying their own performance management goals and development needs (see section 4).

Section 2:
Proformas that assist subject coordinators in their role
Overall objectives

10. To provide the subject coordinators with a checklist to help prioritise their tasks.
11. To assist the coordinator in gaining an overview of what monitoring proformas are available and their reference numbers.
12. To provide a framework for a subject coordinator to write a report about standards in their subject.
13. To assist a subject coordinator in evaluating and reflecting on their current and future role/s.
14. To assist the member of staff in devising their own personal development plan.

Section 3:
Proformas that assist with whole-school strategic planning

These provide a common format on which to record all development areas/issues/concerns which are to emerge as the ongoing school improvement plan.

Of course, many of these proformas can be used by both teacher and subject coordinator.

Overall objectives

Monitoring

15. To give the sequence and overview of key tasks associated with key tools for school improvement.
16. To give an overview of subject teaching observations and the monitoring of work.

Teaching and learning

17. To assist the senior management team with the monitoring of individual teacher appraisal.
18. To help the lesson observer focus on key questions that relate to effective teaching and learning.

Whole-school development

19. To enable governors (or other stakeholders) to get to the core of a problem before raising it as a vague concern at a school meeting.

20. The central proforma for all priorities which links the others together.

The above proformas are set into three sections for convenience and ease of explanation. The categories, however, do overlap and should not be seen as relating to just one section. Each school should put their own interpretation on their use and modify them accordingly.

Also note that the above guides for lesson observations are not suggested as a replacement to existing observation sheets. Over the years many excellent literacy, numeracy and LEA observation sheets (including individual schools' in-house ones) have been devised. You should continue to use the forms that are most relevant and appropriate to your own particular context.

Section 4:

Proformas that assist with collating performance information

Overall objectives

21/22. Prompting sentences. This assists the teacher/subject coordinator in pulling everything together. Other proformas would have helped clarify strengths or weaknesses in both his or her own performance and his subject/s.

23. These questions were devised in order to encapsulate the key issues identified in producing effective teachers. This can be used by individuals as a self-assessment exercise or as part of performance management interview.

Update of professional development

24. Teachers are not always effective in recording their past professional development so this form is a constant reminder. It also reminds staff that visiting colleagues in other classes and/or schools or listening to an inspiring and knowledgeable speaker is all part of their professional development experience.

As a result of the professional development proforma, the teacher/subject coordinator may revisit the subject coordinator proformas, especially 14 – 'My personal development planning sheet' – to help plan his or her future direction.

Section 5:

Can be used by reviewer and reviewee

Overall objectives

Proformas that aid the performance management process

25. To give a format for agreeing objectives at the review meeting

26. To record the jointly agreed planning statement
27. To record the three or four objectives for the performance management cycle

Although performance management is the final part of this section, in reality, the whole process is cyclic and ongoing. All proformas can be incorporated simultaneously and/or in any order chosen by the individual schools.

If you want to see all of the proformas at a glance, there is a summary sheet on page 20. If you want to track the proformas you have distributed amongst your staff there is a tracking sheet on page 21.

Proformas 1-9

Monitoring pupils' work and progress

Proforma 1: Monitoring and presenting pupils' work

Objective
To ensure focused monitoring and consistency in marking pupils' work.
To remind teachers of some key learning information.

This guidance sheet reminds the senior management team and teachers that there is a finite amount of time for marking pupils' work. It is therefore crucial from the outset to clarify and prioritise what will be assessed. Similarly, it releases the busy teacher from being tempted to mark everything.

The second part of the guidance sheet covers key learning issues and encourages the teacher to think about the different ways in which information might be presented to different pupils.

Links to school cycle
This guidance sheet can be introduced at the beginning of a new school year to ensure consistency and focus in whole-school marking. It can be used as a reference at different stages of the year to gauge marking coherence and consistency between teachers, year cohorts, and key stage groups. The guidance can also be used to promote staff discussion on important issues relating to marking and monitoring. This sheet will certainly help to clarify thinking prior to an inspection visit.

Likewise, the second half of the sheet, covering learning styles, can be deployed in a similar way.

Key personnel
Senior management team and/or subject coordinators can use this guidance as part of their whole-school work monitoring role.

In lesson observations, line managers can evaluate how teachers are modifying their teaching to cater for the varying learning styles within their classes.

How this contributes to school improvement
- Ensures whole-school consistency in monitoring pupils' work, a key Ofsted focus.
- Encourages teachers to cater for a variety of learning styles in their teaching.
- More focused marking.
- Sharper and smarter use of teachers' time.
- Encourages more individual learning.

Next steps
- Ensure all teachers adhere to all or part of the guidance.
- Publicise the marking rationale to parents.
- Include this information with other monitoring guidance.
- Begin to construct a learning style profile of all pupils at the school.

(1) Monitoring and presenting pupils' work – including marking guidance

If your objectives are clear then your marking focus will be straightforward. Simply
- identify where the objective/s has/have been achieved
- identify where to give further development/guidance/targets
- keep comments concise, constructive and clear
- a general comment on effort might be useful.

Marking should be strategic, ie. not every piece of work.
It does not have to be whole-class marking.
Oral feedback is more likely to inspire, motivate and clarify misunderstandings.

Encourage pupils to take ownership of future targets, don't let it become a bureaucratic exercise.

Remember, when presenting work, the implications of different learning styles and the difference between right/left brain functions.

Learning styles

The difference between right/left brain function.

	Left	**Right**
	Sequential – from part to whole	Whole picture first
Visual	Critical thinking	Emotion
Auditory	Logic	Space
Kinaesthetic	Analysis	Creativity
	Systems	Images

The brain works by association linking random concepts/ideas/facts into an interconnected network of knowledge. Mind mapping is a good strategy for clarifying concepts and extending ideas.

Remember
- most of the brain's capacity remains unused
- intelligence can be learned
- memory relies on meaning and patterns – the most effective way to learn something new is to see how it relates/builds upon something the child already knows
- emotions trigger in before intellect and can block or enhance learning
- self-motivation is a key to success
- our eating, drinking, exercise, sleeping and all other habits have a direct link on our ability to learn.

Proforma 2: Monitoring basic skills with inclusivity in mind

Objective
To clarify what we mean by inclusivity; raising questions to ensure that there is no underachievement within the school.

With greater emphasis on inclusivity and underachievement (as opposed to attainment) this guidance acts as a prompt to crystallise the school's thinking on monitoring. It reminds the senior management team and subject coordinators/leaders about the rich variety of pupil groupings within the school and raises some key questions.

Links to school cycle
This guidance can be introduced at the beginning of a new school year to ensure all categories of pupil groupings are identified. All data, including key stage tests, ongoing teacher assessment, in-house tests, attendance records, etc. to be linked with the relevant groupings throughout the year.

Key personnel
Senior management and subject coordinators can use this guidance to ensure their monitoring is covering all pupil groupings. The groupings are not exhaustive and some will not be relevant to all schools. Senior management should decide what specific groupings should have top priority for their own school monitoring.

How this contributes to school improvement
Encouraging key personnel to focus on inclusivity and achievement in their own school, a key Ofsted focus.

- Promotes discussion (and therefore greater awareness) between all staff on pupil groupings within the school.
- More focused monitoring.

Next steps
See 'Whole-school monitoring' proforma (3).

This proforma can be used for whole-school monitoring and has further guidance notes.

(2) Monitoring basic skills with inclusivity in mind

We aim to be 'all-inclusive' with regard to educational and social experiences at our school. We celebrate our differences but endeavour to ensure that our variety of backgrounds, situations and circumstances do not lead to individual or groups of pupils underachieving. In short, our aim is to ensure that every child and adult at our school achieves to their full potential in all aspects of their school life.

The following is not an exhaustive list but begins to identify the rich variety of individuals/groups within our school context.

The differences can be as a result of:

- race, gender, special educational needs (including gifted pupils), social/economic background or culture.

There may also be the following categories of pupils/adults within our school:

- those with English as an additional/second language and/or from an ethnic minority background
- those with a disability
- those children in public care or who are young carers
- those who are categorised as travellers or gypsies.

There can, of course, be a combination of the above categories for individuals or groups of children/adults

Ongoing key questions:

- How do standards of achievement compare between the above individuals and groups?
- Is there evidence of underachievement with any individual or group?
- What strategies are being employed to redress the balance?

See: 'Whole-school monitoring' proforma (3).

Proforma 3: Whole-school monitoring

Objective

To record the pupil groupings on a standardised form and highlight other key data about the grouping, so enabling an informative grouping profile to emerge.

The second part of this form is for guidance and can be used as a valuable *aide-mémoire* as well as assisting in identifying the definitive cohort to be monitored.

Links to school cycle

You may decide to incorporate this proforma at the beginning of the school year, as a result of a looming inspection or as a response to data that has identified underachievement with a specific cohort of pupils. On the other hand you may simply wish to use it as a starting point for a staff discussion on monitoring and inclusivity.

Key personnel

Senior management team and subject coordinators for whole-school monitoring.

How this contributes to school improvement

- Ensures monitoring of all groups of pupils in the school.
- Provides an *aide-mémoire* for developing cohort profile and evaluating the work.

Next steps

Ensure all information is passed on to appropriate senior managers, including the special needs coordinator.

After evaluating data and cohort profile, give some thought to whether there are some overlaps with other school groups. For example, is a large proportion of summer-born boys on the SEN register? Are they all British white or are they made up of varying ethnic groups? Conversely, is the higher attaining group made up of autumn-born British white girls?

(3) Whole-school monitoring – focus group proforma

Number of pupils at this school:	
Focus group:	Date:
Percentage whole-school terms:	Number:
Percentage on SEN register:	Number:
Percentage on statements:	Number:
Initials or other identification of focus group/classes:	
Related curriculum targets:	
Notes including review date:	

Evaluating pupils' work

Selecting pupils' work for scrutiny and/or tracing different individuals/cohorts.

Considerations

- **What individuals/cohort do you wish to sample?**

- **Inclusion:** Consider collecting work by different groups.
  (Boys/girls; above average, average and below average; SEN; EAL; age; key stage; different ethnic backgrounds; gifted/talented; social/economic groups; month of birth; pupils with disabilities; pupils in public care and pupils who are carers.)

- **Progress:** The sample should enable you to come to a judgement about progress/improvement over time, so you will need to access work over a period of weeks or across terms/years.

- **Context:** You should be able to place the work in the context of:
  - the syllabus
  - the teacher's planning
  - expected standards/National Curriculum levels.

- **Pupils:** You can learn a lot about standards, and progress in particular, by talking to pupils about the work you have selected. They can give you an indication of how they think they have improved and why.

Proforma 4: Work sampling

Objective
To conduct effective work sampling by scrutinising samples of the work of pupils working at above average, average and below average levels.

The prompt questions and guidance will help to gain a greater insight into the pupils' attitudes to learning, understanding and ability.

Links to school cycle
This proforma can be used throughout the year by a member of the senior management team or subject coordinator/leader while carrying out their monitoring duties.

The questions can also be used by a teacher or teaching assistant to gauge individual, groups or whole-class perceptions, regarding their learning experiences.

Alternatively a school governor might be deployed to ask such questions and give feedback to the relevant staff.

Key personnel
- Senior management team
- Subject coordinator
- Teacher
- Governor

How this contributes to school improvement
Ofsted has found discussing work with pupils to be a very powerful inspection tool. It gives a first-hand insight into teaching and learning, especially when the discussion centres on the pupils' completed work.

If senior managers and subject coordinators ensure this strategy is embedded within their own practice, greater awareness of insights into teaching and learning at the school are likely to emerge.

Next steps
Use the information to feed back to relevant personnel. In future monitoring, ensure existing strengths are built upon and there is improvement in areas that were causing concern.

(4) Work sampling

Three pupils from appropriate class/es working at above average standard, average standard, below average standard and any other relevant category should bring work with them.

General questions might include:

- What did you really enjoy doing?

- Why?

- Tell me about some of the things that you have learned.

- How do you think you are getting on in...?

- What didn't you enjoy doing?

- What things did you find most difficult?

- Why? Etc.

Focus also on specific pieces of work and ask them to tell you about how/why/when they did it, etc.

Other possible questions

Proforma 5: Subject report evaluation sheet

Objective
To obtain a written subject report from a pupil's perspective and additional personal information through interaction with the pupil.

Links to school cycle
This proforma can be used as an evaluation tool after a section/module of work and/or to provide supplementary information for end-of-year reports.

Teachers and subject coordinators could also give a specific cohort and/or whole year group the first part of the proforma to fill out in order to get an instant overview of the pupils' collective learning.

Key personnel
- Subject coordinators
- Teachers

How this contributes to school improvement
- Provides informative feedback for teachers and subject coordinators that can assist with teaching/learning/curriculum evaluation.
- Highlights any inconsistencies between achievement and attitude.

The pupils' attitude towards learning plays an important part in the process of an Ofsted inspection.

Next steps
- Pass on the information to the relevant members of staff.
- Ensure description of completed work is consistent with the school's programme of study.
- Log the attitude and other personal grades for future monitoring to see if there is an upward or downward trend.

(5) Subject report evaluation sheet – pupil's perspective

Subject .... Year ....

Term .... Name ....

I have completed some work on

I have learned

Other comments

Adult evaluation after discussion with pupils

	Poor				Excellent
Attitude	1	2	3	4	5
Confidence	1	2	3	4	5
Motivation	1	2	3	4	5
Attention	1	2	3	4	5
Applying subject?	1	2	3	4	5

(only grade if appropriate)

Proforma 6: Class survey

Objective
To gauge the pupils' responses before the official letters and/or questionnaires are sent out at the time of the next Ofsted inspection.

To familiarise and clarify meaning for pupils so they can answer future questions more confidently.

To give valuable feedback for the class teacher.

Links to school cycle
As the above indicates this would be a useful preliminary exercise before the official Ofsted inspection. It can also provide the class teacher with an insight into how individuals, groups or even the whole class is feeling. Completing them towards the end of each term might prove useful and enable the teacher to gauge upward and downward trends in pupils' perceptions. Over a longer term (two to three years) it would be fascinating to compare results.

Key personnel
- Class teacher

How this contributes to school improvement
If Ofsted finds similar information useful, then it is certainly helpful to class teachers by:

- giving valuable insight into how pupils view the class ethos and organisation
- encouraging the teacher to take stock and celebrate what they are doing well: success breeds success
- ensuring the teacher has no 'blind spots' and is presented with areas that might need improving.

Next steps
The teacher reflects on both strengths and points to develop and notes them on proformas 21–22 (prompting sentences proformas) as appropriate.

(6) Class survey

We are going to conduct our own class survey. Please answer all questions honestly. Please don't write only what you think teachers want to hear. Your answers could be different from your friends'.

	Yes	Don't know	No
I am happy to be in my class			
I know what the learning objectives are for most lessons			
I enjoy coming to school			
My teacher enjoys teaching			
I think my school rules are fair			
There is usually an adult to help me when I'm stuck			
I feel safe at school			
I am always expected to work hard in class			
There is always a helpful adult to talk to at school			
Most of my class concentrate on their work			
I know my target/s			
I know what to do to achieve my targets			
My teacher usually has time for me			
Homework helps my learning			
My work is usually marked			
We always celebrate good work in class			
I know a little about the different ways children learn			
All the children in my class get on with each other			
All the children in my school usually get on with each other			
My class is usually an exciting place to learn in			
My time at school usually goes by quickly			
My parents/carers know how to help me with school work			
I enjoy playtimes and dinnertimes			
I enjoy the school assemblies			

The best thing about my school is
_____
_____

My school would be better if
_____
_____

Proforma 7: Expectation sheet

Objective
To provide a class/year group expectation profile very quickly from which future target-setting data can be produced.

Links to school cycle
A whole-school audit can take place using this proforma to evaluate how different year groups are progressing. This can be another source of information prior to setting pupil targets. This sheet can also cover individual subjects, especially for literacy and numeracy targets.

The proformas can be completed by using pupils' initials and/or straightforward numbers. The only pupils who are not recorded are those working at or above the expected level. This proforma is particularly useful in identifying pupils who are slightly below the expected level, where a minimal increase of resources might have a big impact on overall attainment.

The information on this proforma can be used in conjunction with proforma 9, 'SATs predictions'.

Key personnel
- Senior management team
- Subject coordinators
- Teachers

How this contributes to school improvement
The simplicity of this proforma enables the relevant personnel to see at an instant how a cohort of pupils is progressing without having to wade through a large amount of numerical data.

This enables appropriate personnel to make quick and informal decisions about future strategies and the targets of resources.

The proforma can provide valuable monitoring/tracking information for senior managers if it is completed on a regular termly/yearly cycle.

The above approach will ensure that the school has qualitative information on which to base realistic but challenging pupil targets. Such an approach will provide quality evaluative data for Ofsted.

Next steps
By calculating the percentage of pupils who are not included on the proforma (because they are at or above the expected level) you are left with the percentage that are below the expected level. Similarly if you include those pupils who are only 'slightly below' those at or above the expected level you can assess how significant such an upward shift would be to school statistics. This information will be very useful to the senior management team.

(7) Expectation sheet

Class .... Year ....

Children working below their expected level in (subject)

a) Slightly below

b) Below

c) Substantially below

Strategies to counter underachievement

No. in class   Usual time of lesson

Calculations

If A achieve =

If B achieve =

If C achieve =

Proforma 8: Attitude/progress sheet

Objective
To provide an instant pupil profile snapshot covering effort, achievement and personal information.

Links to school cycle
This proforma provides supplementary information for the school's termly or annual report. It can also be used as part of the school's routine monitoring on groups of pupils.

The collation of both personal attributes and academic progress can be valuable information for the school and Ofsted's inclusive agenda.

Key personnel
- Senior management team
- Subject coordinator
- Teacher

How this contributes to school improvement
This form can highlight anomalies in effort and achievement. For example, if a pupil is achieving at B and only scores C for effort, questions might be asked about the pupil's lack of motivation and how to improve effort so as to increase performance.

Other personal attributes can also be assessed and pupils with similar profiles, for instance those who score low with their listening skills, might be placed on an in-house development programme.

Next steps
Look for potential correlations in the data, for example, between low achievement and poor listening scores, or between low achievement and poor communication skills and so on.

Using these forms at regular intervals might highlight, for example, that moving from a steady to improving trend is often accompanied by a significant improvement in one or more of the personal attributes scores. This information, set in the context of your own school, will be extremely useful to the appropriate personnel.

(8) Attitude/progress sheet

Subject .... Year ....

Date .... Name ....

	Poor				Excellent
Confidence	1	2	3	4	5
Motivation	1	2	3	4	5
Listening	1	2	3	4	5
Communication	1	2	3	4	5

Effort	Achievement	Trend
A	A	**Improving**
B	B	
C	C	**Steady**
D	D	
E	E	**More application needed**

Comments

Proforma 9: SATs predictions

Objective

To provide an instant snapshot (best and worst case scenarios) for SATs predictions in English, mathematics and science.

To highlight where related information can be found.

Links to school cycle

This proforma can be incorporated at any time during the school year. It gives the senior management team and teacher a clear overview of SATs predictions. There is no need to wait until the actual year of the SATs to complete this form; using it in the preceding year/s can highlight strengths and weaknesses.

The information on this proforma can be used in conjunction with the 'Expectation sheet' proforma (7).

Key personnel

- Senior management team
- Subject coordinators
- Teacher

How this contributes to school improvement

If the proforma is incorporated as a regular part of school monitoring and well before the SATs period, it can highlight areas that may need attention and leave a realistic timescale to take appropriate action. If it is used in conjunction with 'Expectation sheet' proforma (7), the senior management team gain further detail and greater insight into the overall situation.

Next steps

Start to cross-reference the 'related information' in order to gain an accurate and realistic year group profile.

Review 'Expectation sheet' proforma (7) and reconsider whether your predictions are too cautionary or optimistic.

(9) SATs predictions

Name of teacher (current and previous)		
Year 2 SATs	**Year 6 SATs**	**Results:**
Percentage achieving level .... in		

Subject	Best case scenario	Worst case scenario
English		
Mathematics		
Science		

Related information	
No. IEPs	
Previous: QCA optional SATs results	
Relevant in-house test information	
Teacher assessment/evidence	
Baseline assessment or otherwise	

Comments

Optimus Education

Proformas 10-14

Assisting the subject coordinators in their role

Proforma 10: Subject coordinators' checklist

Objective

To provide the subject coordinators with a checklist to help prioritise their tasks.

Links to school cycle

The school improvement plan will dictate the tasks that are currently most/least important. In addition there may be some subjects that are left on the back-burner for a while because they have had recent scrutiny and/or others have been given a high priority through the school's own self-evaluation or through other external agencies, such as Ofsted.

Key personnel

- Senior management team
- Subject coordinators

How this contributes to school improvement

The form identifies key tasks that effective schools should carry out. They are not exhaustive, but if they are being covered in all subjects within a given time frame it is almost definite that school improvement is taking place on a broad scale.

Next steps

Many of the tasks correlate with proformas in the coordinators, monitoring, performance management and whole-school development sections; the permutations are too numerous to list here.

A good starting point, in consultation with your line manager, would be to select the appropriate proformas from the overall pack in order to gauge the breadth and depth of the tasks over a short-, medium- and long-term perspective.

(10) Subject coordinators' checklist

Name	Date	Subject/focus
Compiling/updating portfolio		
Check planning and its links to learning		
Team teaching		
Lesson observation		
Policy review		
Reviewing/ordering resources		
Evaluate standards/achievements		
Course attendance		
Leading colleagues		
Organising INSET		
Promoting cross-curricular links		
Liaising parent/governors		
Monitor pupils' work		
Activity relating to raising standards		
Specific knowledge update		
Other		

Notes

Proforma 11: Subject coordinators' summary of monitoring

Objective
To assist the coordinator in gaining an overview of what monitoring proformas are available and their reference numbers.

Links to school cycle
Monitoring pupils' work has always been an important part of the subject coordinator's role.

The school development plan should highlight which subjects have been given the highest priority and which aspects of the subject need attention.

This is likely to dictate the monitoring focus and future strategy.

Key personnel
- School management team
- Subject coordinators

How this contributes to school improvement
Whole-school monitoring is a broad description that on the one hand can seem too vast for one person to manage, yet on the other hand too vague and general to have a specific impact on school improvement.

The proformas assist the subject coordinator in dealing with this uncertainty by breaking up monitoring into several strands. The proformas will assist with school improvement because they are streamlined, focused, easy to use and will provide specific information that can be evaluated to inform future progress.

Next steps
Share all monitoring information with your line manager and other coordinators at appropriate times. It can be very informative to see how individuals and groups of pupils perform in different subjects.

Their attitude towards different subjects may also raise interesting questions. Does monitoring indicate that pupils have strengths and weaknesses/likes/dislikes in different subjects, or is it also to do with the teaching of such subjects?

(11) Subject coordinators' summary of monitoring

Activity:	Proforma numbers	Action taken/date
Marking of pupils' work	1	
Monitoring of inclusivity	2	
Evaluating pupils' work	3, 4, 5 and 8	
Evaluating pupils' attitudes	6 and 8	
Evaluating future standards	7 and 9	
Other information		

Proforma 12: Improving standards

Objective
To provide a framework for a subject coordinator to write a report about standards in their subject.

All too often subject reports are too general, this guidance ensures the report focuses on standards and achievement.

Links to school cycle
See 'Subject coordinators' summary of monitoring' proforma (11).

Proforma 11 can direct the coordinator to specific proformas that will assist with this report on standards.

Key personnel
- Subject coordinators

How this contributes to school improvement
The framework of this proforma ensures the focus is on standards/achievement and because of this it does not become a general unfocused report.

Two sections of the report specifically cover how development work has improved standards and how future development work will improve standards in the future.

Next steps
Share the report with your line manager.

Reflect whether development work carried out to improve standards in your own subject could be transferred to other areas of the curriculum in order to spread the improvement to other subjects.

(12) Improving standards

Improving standards in .... (subject)

Brief report

Current standards/achievement (including specific cohorts of pupils year/key stage groups, etc.)

Recent development work and how this has improved standards

Future development work and how this will improve standards

Other comments

Proforma 13: Self-appraisal for subject coordinators

Objective

To assist a subject coordinator in evaluating and reflecting on their current and future role/s.

Links to school cycle

The ideal time to complete this proforma is prior to a performance management interview with a line manager.

Key personnel

- Subject coordinator

How this contributes to school improvement

This ensures that the subject coordinator's responsibilities and aspirations are not overlooked by their line manager. Information on this proforma may highlight future possibilities that the line manager had not considered. Whenever practicable, if information on this sheet is acted upon in a positive way, staff are more likely to feel valued, resulting in a likely increase in both motivation and performance.

Next steps

Whenever possible these proformas should be considered collectively because if acted upon, each individual outcome will have a knock-on effect on overall staffing responsibilities.

(13) Self-appraisal for subject coordinators

Name ....

Current responsibilities/subject

Responsibilities/subjects prepared to take on

Extra-curricular offerings

Other comments

Proforma 14: My personal development planning sheet

Objective

To assist the member of staff in devising their own personal development plan.

Links to school cycle

This is likely to be completed after or during a performance management interview with line manager.

Key personnel

- Teacher
- Subject coordinator
- Senior management team

How this contributes to school improvement

This proforma assists with personal/professional development.

Developing and investing in staff is an integral part of school improvement not least because it will unlock staff potential and increase individual performance.

Next steps

Line managers should regularly scan these proformas and take note of the various headings to ensure that the plan remains dynamic.

For example, at any time during planning ask such questions as:

- Is progress to date, within the overall timescale, sufficient?
- Are appropriate resources being made available?
- Do the personnel identified as supporting this plan have sufficient experience, expertise and the personal qualities required?

(14) My personal development planning sheet

Priority

Target

Success criteria

Tasks

Time scale

Personnel to support me

Resources I will need

Monitoring review – how/who?

Evaluation

Miscellaneous notes

Proformas 15-20

Whole-school strategic planning

Proforma 15: Strategies for monitoring educational standards

Objective

To give the sequence and overview of key tasks associated with key tools for school improvement.

The list is not exhaustive but simply an *aide-mémoire* for starting points in school improvement work.

Links to school cycle

It is likely that the previous teaching/learning and/or subject coordinator proformas have already identified the issues and the way forward for you and your team.

However you arrived at your decision, once the tasks and tools have been decided upon, ensure you communicate all key aspects to the appropriate audiences. The last section of proforma 15 reminds you of opportunities for doing this.

Proforma 20, entitled 'School development', is a useful proforma to communicate and action whole-school planning.

Key personnel
- Senior management team
- Subject coordinators

How this contributes to school improvement

Assists the senior management team in strategic thinking while ensuring joined-up thinking and effective communication with a variety of stakeholders.

Next steps

Once decisions have been made about the sequence of key tasks and associated tools to be employed, thought should be given about staff/governor meeting airtime, use of professional development days and, if appropriate, what issues should be communicated to parents.

(15) Strategies for monitoring educational standards

Key tasks

- Identify the subject/s in which the school needs to improve
- Analyse the areas/aspects causing concern
- Ascertain whether a whole-school/key stage/year group problem
- Develop curriculum targets and related success criteria
- Prioritise key objectives
- Identify key personnel
- Evaluate resources available
- Implement monitoring and evaluation strategies.

Key tools

- Senior management team
- In-house monitoring data
- Other schools
- PANDA
- Autumn package
- SATs results (including optional and other tests)
- Baseline data
- Exemplification booklets
- Pupils' work (including prior attainment); category of pupil
- Robust planning/assessment, marking and monitoring policies/procedures.

Essential link-ups to enhance joined-up thinking and communicate goals/visions

- School development plan/Standards fund
- Performance management policy/procedures
- Whole-school staff meetings
- Governor meetings/working parties
- Parents' meetings/newsletters/assemblies
- Community: newspapers/school brochure.

Proforma 16: Subject priorities

Objective
To give an overview of subject teaching observations and the monitoring of work.

Links to school cycle
This proforma enables the senior management team to gain a clear overview of the tasks covered by the subject coordinator/leader. There may be valid reasons why some subjects have not been highlighted on this form. Remember, subject coordinators and their line managers may have referred to proformas 10–14 in order to prioritise or reprioritise work on specific subjects.

Key personnel
- Senior management team

How this contributes to school improvement
This proforma highlights gaps in teaching observations and work monitoring in different subject areas, thus ensuring no subjects are overlooked. If there are gaps, it is because of the school's priorities and not due to an oversight.

Next steps
If there are gaps in subject areas, ensure it is due to the planned priorities and discuss the gaps with the appropriate personnel.

(16) Subject priorities

Subject	Teaching observed	Work monitored (Year group)	Next steps
English			
Mathematics			
Science			
ICT			
RE			
PSHE			
History			
Geography			
Music			
Art			
D & T			
PE			

Proforma 17: Teacher appraisal/monitoring

Objective

To assist the senior management team with the monitoring of individual teacher appraisal.

This sheet is designed to be an ongoing summary record of appraisal for individual teachers.

Links to school cycle

Information for this proforma can be lifted from the relevant teaching and learning proformas 1–9 and subject coordinator proformas 10–14.

Key personnel

- Senior management team
- Head

How this contributes to school improvement

This proforma encourages the appraisal process to be ongoing as opposed to a one-off event. Continual development in small regular steps is more likely to have a greater impact on staff/school improvement than an annual or bi-annual snapshot of performance.

The final section of the proforma is completed by both parties in discussion with the head, so that the appraisal process itself can be monitored in order to ensure its ongoing effectiveness.

Next steps

Review the proforma in conjunction with the relevant teaching and learning proformas 1–9 and/or subject coordinator proformas 10–14. Proforma 14, 'My personal development planning sheet', may be particularly useful.

(17) Teacher appraisal/monitoring

Name .... Date ....

The teacher: Classroom practice	
• Demonstrates and applies effective teaching/learning with all pupils including differentiated work with a whole class, group and individual pupils (See Ofsted/literacy/numeracy lesson observation proformas).	**1 2 3 4 5 6**
• Readily identifies issues that need addressing.	**1 2 3 4 5 6**
• Demonstrates ability to plan, organise and implement necessary action.	**1 2 3 4 5 6**
• Able to review progress based on appropriate and accurate data.	**1 2 3 4 5 6**
• The class is orderly and disciplined with a purposeful atmosphere.	**1 2 3 4 5 6**
• Other adults are being used effectively.	**1 2 3 4 5 6**

Appraiser comment

Pupils' work	
• Work handed in is of a reasonable/high standard and completed.	**1 2 3 4 5 6**
• Marking is consistent with productive feedback when appropriate.	**1 2 3 4 5 6**
• The presentation is of a good standard.	**1 2 3 4 5 6**
• Work is at the expected standard or above.	**1 2 3 4 5 6**
• Work covers appropriate National Curriculum programmes of study.	**1 2 3 4 5 6**
• Homework is used effectively to raise standards and is consistent with the school policy.	**1 2 3 4 5 6**

Appraiser comment

Other professional aspects	
• Good understanding of own subject/specialism.	**1 2 3 4 5 6**
• Work is well planned.	**1 2 3 4 5 6**
• The teacher ensures he/she has ongoing professional development.	**1 2 3 4 5 6**
• The teacher is seen as a support for colleagues.	**1 2 3 4 5 6**

Appraiser comment

To be completed with head	
Appraisal must:	
• Affect classroom practice in a positive way.	**1 2 3 4 5 6**
• Be manageable/minimal paperwork.	**1 2 3 4 5 6**
• Seen to be worth the effort by both parties.	**1 2 3 4 5 6**
• Be ongoing.	**1 2 3 4 5 6**

Rating 1 = Excellent, 6 = Poor

Proforma 18: Teaching and learning observations

Objective

To help the lesson observer focus on key questions that relate to effective teaching and learning.

Links to school cycle

Information could be transferred to the 'Teacher appraisal/monitoring' (17), 'Subject priorities' (16) or 'My personal development planning sheet' (14) proformas.

Key personnel

- Senior management team.

How this contributes to school improvement

Teaching and learning is at the heart of school improvement and this proforma ensures this is the focus. It is useful to give a copy of this proforma to those being observed so they can reflect on their own practice before the actual observations.

Next steps

See above links.

Rehearse the feedback session using the questions as prompts. Your lesson observation feedback should be to the point, clear and backed up by evidence. It is useful to highlight:

- what went well and why this was so
- what could be better and how this might be achieved.

If there are any real concerns then a dialogue with the appropriate personnel may need to take place. You may suggest that the observed teacher completes 'My personal development planning sheet' proforma (14) with you.

(18) Teaching and learning observations

- What are the lesson objectives?
- Has the teacher made the objectives clear from the outset?
- Are the lesson objectives appropriate for all pupils?
- Have appropriate resources been developed and made accessible to pupils?
- Does the teaching methodology cater for the range of individuals within the group?
- Is ICT being effectively incorporated into the lesson?
- Is appropriate differentiation incorporated?
- Are all pupils treated equally and included throughout the lessons?
- Are pupils engaged?
- Are pupils sufficiently challenged?
- Do they understand what is expected of them?
- Are they learning?
- Is the lesson well organised?
- Are other adults being deployed effectively?

After the lesson, through observation, talking to pupils and scrutinising work, ask yourself the following questions

- Have the learning objectives been met by all (almost all) pupils?
- Was this lesson unsatisfactory? Why?
- Was this lesson satisfactory? Why?
- Was this lesson good? Why?
- Was this lesson very good/excellent? Why?

Give at least two clear reasons for the above judgements, including two reasons why it didn't make the next grade

Proforma 19: Governing body

Objective
To enable governors (or other stakeholders) to get to the core of a problem before raising it as a vague concern at a school meeting.

Links to school cycle
This form can be used throughout the year and/or leading up to formal meetings where problems/concerns are discussed. If, having got to the core of the problem, a decision is made to add it to the school improvement plans, then the starting point would be the 'School development' proforma (20).

Key personnel
- Senior management team
- Governors
- Other stakeholders

How this contributes to school improvement
The proforma not only enables those adopting it to get to the core issues more quickly but saves a great deal of preliminary discussion, which often finds key stakeholders going round in circles.

The time and energy saved using this proforma allows for more focus on the central issues of school improvement.

Next steps
If the issue is deemed worthy of further investigation, transfer information to 'School development' proforma (20).

(19) Governing body

Dealing with issues in school

What is the problem?

Why is it a problem?

Evidence that the problem exists.

What do I suggest we do about the problem?

Agreed action after consultation with headteacher.

Does it need to be raised at a governors' meeting?

Yes? Please see chair at least three days before meeting.

Proforma 20: School development

Objective

The central proforma for all priorities which links the others together.

A common format on which to record all development areas/issues/concerns that are to emerge as the ongoing school improvement plan.

Links to school cycle

The different boxes can be cross-referenced to the appropriate heading on other proformas. For example, if the teaching of a specific subject is identified as a particular weakness, this might be cross-referenced to the 'Subject coordinators' checklist' (10), 'Improving standards' (12), 'Subject priorities' (16) and so on. Such proformas may or may not confirm that such weaknesses exist.

Key personnel

Any stakeholders who are entrusted by the senior management team or governors to have input into the school improvement plans.

How this contributes to school improvement

A well constructed proforma will give a clear direction in all aspects of school improvement.

The advantage of using loose leaf proformas is that they are easily duplicated and key personnel can have instant access to them.

In addition, unlike school improvement folders or documents, all aspects of school improvement can be worked on, updated and cross-referenced simultaneously and with ease.

Next steps

Collate all 'School development' proformas, proforma (20) and prioritise in categories A, B and C.

A = Action

B = Brewing

C = Coming up.

(20) School development

Priority

Target

Success criteria

Task/s

Timescale	Personnel	Resources
Monitoring and review	**Evaluation**	**Miscellaneous notes**

Proformas 21-24

Collating performance information

Proformas 21 and 22: Prompting sentences

Objective
Prompting sentences/alternative prompting.

To encourage a constructive performance management dialogue by suggesting prompt statements/questions.

Links to school cycle
Numerous proformas can be used in the above dialogue. Part of the preliminary discussions will centre on which proformas to incorporate in order to achieve a constructive and balanced dialogue.

Key personnel
- Senior management team
- Teacher

How this contributes to school improvement
Ensures a well balanced and fluid discussion based on evidence via the proformas. This should contribute to constructive outcomes which should have a positive effect on school improvement.

Next steps
Consider completing 'My personal development planning sheet' proforma (14).

(21) Prompting sentences – Sheet 1

1. I feel my greatest strength as a teacher is...

2. I am happiest in my work when...

3. The aspect of my work I have been most pleased about this year is...

4. I feel my most significant contribution to the school this year has been...

5. I feel my greatest weakness as a teacher is...

6. I feel the children I teach would benefit more from what I do if...

7. I feel the least successful aspect of my work over the last year has been...

8. My main targets for next year are...

9. The help I most need from the school is...

10. In two years' time, I see myself...

11. In ten years' time, I see myself...

12. I love teaching because...

(22) Alternative prompting – Sheet 2

1. Which aspects of your work do you feel especially pleased with?

2. Which aspects of your work have not gone as well as you might have hoped?

3. Are there any constraints or difficulties you are working under?

4. In what ways do you want to develop your work in the coming year?

5. What training or new skills do you think you need in the coming year?

Proforma 23: Continuous professional development for teachers

Objective
To provide 20 key questions for self-assessment/professional development that gets to the heart of teaching and learning.

The questions were selected after reflecting on effective practice based on research and evidence.

Links to school cycle
The questions may highlight gaps in practice and/or professional development and these can be noted on other proformas such as 'My personal development planning sheet' proforma (14).

Key personnel
- Senior management team
- Teachers

How this contributes to school improvement
The 20 questions encourage self-evaluation; as with school self-evaluation, this is an integral part of the improvement process.

Next steps
- Highlight priorities for improving practice.
- Highlight gaps in training and development.
- Try to ensure practice priorities and development complement each other.

(23) Continuous professional development for teachers

The 20 definitive questions regarding

- performance management/appraisal
- Ofsted
- threshold assessment.

1. Are you aware how you use body language in your teaching? Stillness, gestures, mannerisms, movement/relaxed posture, etc.
2. Are you aware how you use voice in your teaching? (Volume, pace, tone.)
3. Are you aware of your questioning style and techniques?
4. Are your expectations appropriate and challenging?
5. How do you ensure your own subject knowledge is secure?
6. Is your planning sound, purposeful and clear?
7. What use do you make of prior learning experiences/data?
8. Are you clear about what completed work should look like?
9. Is your teaching and assessment differentiated and focused?
10. Is your marking specific and informative?
11. Is your feedback directional?
12. Do you use objectives/targets to motivate the pupils?
13. Do you use homework as a natural back-up/progression to class work?
14. Is your class organised and set up to maximise teaching and learning?
15. How do you deploy your classroom assistant to ensure maximum benefits?
16. How do you make optimal use of educational resources?
17. How do you greet your class in the mornings, returning from break/lunchtime?
18. What strategy do you incorporate/adopt to ensure continuous professional development?
19. How do you support your colleagues?
20. What other questions do you need to ask in order to challenge your performance?

Proforma 24: Summary of CPD for individual teachers

Objective
To provide a summary of professional development for individual teachers.

Links to school cycle
The proforma should provide supplementary information for the performance management dialogue.

Key personnel
- Senior management team
- Teachers

How this contributes to school improvement
The summary of professional development will enable the teacher and school management team to highlight any gaps in the teachers' development/training, ensuring that all teachers receive a broad and balanced development programme. Effective and balanced professional development is more likely to enhance school improvement.

Next steps
Copies of these forms, completed by individual teachers, will be handed to the head so that he or she can monitor professional development of the whole staff.

- Highlight priorities for improving practice.
- Highlight gaps in training and development.
- Try to ensure practice priorities and development complement each other.

(24) Summary of CPD for individual teachers

Initials	Subject/theme/topic	Dates

Proformas 25-27

Performance management

Proformas 25 and 27: Performance management

To assist with clear linkage between this publication and the latest performance management regulations please see over leaf.

i. The review meeting

ii. The planning statement/s

iii. The objectives

The school should use this publication in conjunction with its own performance management policy (Sept 07) and its related pay policy.

(25) The review meeting

i. The review meeting

Below are some of the key areas that should be covered in this meeting.

Ensure all evidence/documents/data are at hand for this meeting including the relevant job description.

This is a two-way professional dialogue reflecting on the last performance cycle and looking forward to the next one. Issues that affected past performance (positive or negative) and which may also affect future performances are identified.

Planned support in the past is reviewed and future support is considered. Previous professional development is evaluated and future needs are discussed.

Judgements should focus on how far performance criteria have been met.

Looking to the future – key questions for the next cycle

What would you like to achieve within the context of whole school improvement?

What would you like to achieve within your professional/personal context?

How do you see your career developing over the next year/next five years?

See also Prompting sentences (Proforma (21))

Agree classroom observation date/s

Objectives should focus on school/professional priorities. They should be time bound, challenging but achievable. Some objectives may be achievable within the performance management cycle whilst others may require a longer time span, in which case clear progress benchmarks should be agreed from the outset.

(26) The planning statement/s

ii. Planning statement/s

Relating to the current cycle of performance management

Reviewer	Date
Reviewee	**Date**
Pay/Conditions Implications	**Date**

Signed Reviewer ………………………….   Signed Reviewee …………………………..

Key Related Proformas

(12) Improving standards

(13) Self-appraisal for subject coordinators

(14) My personal development planning sheet

(17) Teacher appraisal/monitoring

(18) Teaching and learning observations

(20) School development

(21) Prompting sentences-sheet 1

(23) Continuous professional development for teachers

(24) Summary of CPD for individual teachers

(27) The objectives

iii. The objectives

Appraiser .... Appraisee .... Date ....

Objective	Success criteria
Time Scale	
Objective	Success criteria
Time Scale	
Objective	Success criteria
Time Scale	
Objective	Success criteria
Time Scale	

To identify:
- Resources/strategies
- Professional development
- Links to school improvement
- Other related issues

Further reading

The Mind Map Book, Tony Buzan, Barry Buzan.
GP Putnams, 1996.
ISBN 0452273226.

The Numbers Game: the use of assessment data in primary and secondary schools by Ofsted inspectors, K Hedger and D Jesson.
Centre for performance evaluation and resource management, University of York, 1999.
ISBN 0953629910.

Leading the Learning School, Colin Weatherley.
Network Education Press, 2000.
ISBN 1855390701.

Leadership and the One Minute Manager, K Blanchard, P Zigarri, D Zigarri.
Quill, 2000.
ISBN 0688163556.

The Power of Positive Thinking, Norman Vincent Peale.
Simon and Schuster, 2003.
ISBN 0743234804.

School Self-evaluation Guidance, Cambridgeshire LEA.
Cambridge County Council, 2003.
ISBN 1904452078.

Excellence and Enjoyment: Learning and teaching in the primary years. Assessment for learning.
DfES 2004. Ref DfES 0521-2004 G

Excellence and Enjoyment: Learning and teaching in the primary years. Continuing professional development.
DfES 2004. Ref DfES 0344-2004 G

Speaking, Listening, Learning: working with children in Key Stages 1 and 2.
DfES 2004. Ref. DfES 0163-2004

The Seven Habits of Highly Effective People, Stephen R Covey.
Simon and Schuster, 2005.
ISBN 0743268164.